Bliss

Conscious

Communication

*Transmuting Ordinary Chats
Into Extraordinary Conversations*

A Co-Creation
By Happy and _____

Published & Distributed by:
Books For Earthlings
Books_For_Earthlings@hotmail.com
The Haven of Well-Being
Tryphena RD 1
Great Barrier Island
New Zealand (Aotearoa)
(09) 429 0122

Bliss Conscious Communication is the author's response to oodles of wondrous friends who have exclaimed, "Happy! You blissball! You cheery starburst...!" then sometimes asked, "What's your secret?"

May all beings live in harmonious bliss.
For more blissformation, email: happyatthehaven@xtra.co.nz

ISBN: 0-473-09766-4

A Prophecy

Bliss consciously we shall speak
With every brilliant ray of our being.
And when listening is deemed
Sacred once more,
Communication will return
To communion.

Aware that each word wields
The power of the universe,
Able to perceive that every utterance
Is etched as if in fire across the sky,
We will rediscover
That even one thought expressed,
Yes, even a single word
Changes the world forever.

Dedication

To the Pan-Planetary Enjoyment of
Bliss Conscious Communication
Because Our Mouths
Are Meant To Be
Sanctuaries

Your Dedication

How To Absorb Every Iota Of Bliss From This Book

Bliss Conscious Communication beams with brilliant quotes, *your* quotes! On every page await opportunities to create uplifting responses uniquely yours. With blissipline, we will author herein a treasure trove of rip-roaring queries and inspiring proclamations. Feel free to quote yourself!

Does your *commun*ication foster *commun*ion? It is intended to! *Commun*ication and *commun*ion are rooted in the word *commune*, which originally meant 'together become one'.

Words are our commonest gifts. With words we colour and sculpt our worlds. We are what we think, say and do, so why verbally hobble when we can boogaloo?

While we are yet alive, may we thrive by making magic of everyday conversations. Let the alchemy begin.

Bliss
Conscious
Communication

Transmuting Ordinary Chats
Into Extraordinary Conversations

A Co-Creation
By Happy and _____

Your Fore Words

To begin, let's jump in by considering a few views regarding communication. For instance,

In discussions, which subjects especially delight you?

☼

☼

What most entices you to listen?

☼

☼

What most frequently inspires you to speak?

☼

☼

Which purposes for communicating do you feel are among the most beneficial?

☼

☼

What is it about certain conversations which leave you feeling particularly satisfied?

☼

☼

Questioning Common Questions

According to a recent survey these are the seven most frequently asked questions in the English language:

1. How are you?
2. What's your name?
3. What time is it?
4. Where are you from?
5. What do you do?
6. How old are you?
7. What do you want to do?

Do the above questions inspire you? They certainly didn't inspire me. Upon realizing this, I began to wonder, *why do we ask what we ask?* What is the impact of the most common questions that we ask?

Questions are important! Approximately one quarter of our conversations entail asking questions, and two quarters entail answering those questions. Questions are worthy of scrutiny and exultation!

Before asking anything of anyone, what if we were to first quietly question our questions in order to evaluate the worth of the questions we are about to ask? What would these pre-question questions be? Here are a few possibilities:

Does this question accentuate the positive?
Could this question lead to something wonderful?
What questions can I ask that honour our highest aspirations?

Before asking a question, which questions could you ask yourself?

☼

☼

☼

The Fabulous Five

It is our questions, not our answers,
which most influence our lives.

Which five questions do you most frequently ask others?

1. How are you

2. Where are you from

3.

4.

5.

Which kind of response does each of these highly influential questions tend to generate in you and in others?

1.

2.

3.

4.

5.

Feel free to erase and modify these answers
as you experiment and feel inspired.

Blissful Beginnings

Does the question "How are you" inspire you? It could!

"How are you?" provides a golden opportunity to decide and define how one feels, and, if one is enthusiastic enough, to uplift the conversational tone by transmuting mediocre responses such as *Okay* and *Not Bad* into creative bursts of joy. Here are several options to play with while you concoct a multitude of gleeful beauties of your own.

How are you? How am I? I'm …

☼ Content beyond measure. ☼ Grateful to be here with you. ☼ Jubilant. ☼ Yes. ☼ In love. In love with life. ☼ Delighted. ☼ Truly. ☼ Gorgeous. ☼ Absolutely fabulous. ☼ Incredibly blessed. ☼ Scintillating. ☼ Divine. ☼ Sublime. ☼ Effulgent. ☼ Splendid. ☼ Kaleidoscopic. ☼ Whistling. ☼ Today is the finest day of my life, and this is the finest moment. ☼ Humbled to be living amidst angels like you. ☼ Truly blossoming. ☼ A song's in my heart. ☼ Supremely glorious. ☼ Legendary. ☼Blithe. ☼ Dedicated. ☼ Soothing. ☼ Loamy. ☼ Sprouting. Panoramic. ☼ Glad. ☼ Breezy. ☼Partly cloudy with a chance of sprinkles in the afternoon. ☼ Frolicking. ☼ Slowly. ☼ Enjoying this moment to the utmost. ☼ Invigorated. ☼ Serene. ☼ Terribly good. ☼ Thriving. ☼ Singing. ☼ Charming. ☼ In awe. ☼ Feeling optimistic, thank you. And you?

How are *you*?

☼ in love with life ☼ feeling happy

☼ splendid ☼ supremely glorious

☼ ☼ optimistic

New Bliss Queries

Since the ho-hum commonality of the question "How are you?" sometimes elicits less-than-fabulous responses, let's concoct our own bliss-dipped questions. Merry queries evoke delightful responses. Knowing this, we can create uplifting new alternatives, such as these:

What especially delighted you today?
What interesting things have you been exploring?
Who has been inspiring you these days?
Why are you feeling especially grateful?
What uplifting news would you like to share?
What do you love about your job? home? life? self? nose?
What are your dreams? How are you manifesting these dreams?
How is your spectrum of reality expanding?
Which wise/funny/inspiring insights have you been entertaining?
Who or what do you find particularly endearing, and why?
What's the central focus of your enthusiasm these days?
What intriguing concepts have you been exploring lately?
What do you value most?
What's your healthiest (kindest, oddest, sublimest...) habit?
How do you best tap your unlimited potential?
Which virtues do you most admire in people, and why?
What do you aspire to?
Would you venture to share some inspirational highlights of your autobiography?
What's the bliss?

The word question is rooted in *quest*, which means "to seek, to search for; an adventurous expedition". Questions were originally posed in the spirit of a quest. Let us reinstate the tradition.

Your Bliss Queries

Which questions would you create to inspire joy in others? (What would *you* enjoy being asked? What are *you* most interested in knowing?)) For inspirational hints, feel free to gather from the bliss query verbs below.

☼ *How has someone encouraged you today?*

☼ *What do you admire in others*

☼

☼

☼

☼

Bliss Query Verbs

Abide, admire, ascend, aspire, celebrate, concentrate, create, discover, enhance, empower, encourage, expand, explore, express, enrich, enthuse, free, heighten, honour, illuminate, imagine, infuse, include, intuit, liberate, meditate, nourish, realise, serve, share, unite, wonder...

Which words of movement move *you* most?

☼   ☼   ☼

Exuberant Endearments

What if, suddenly, on the brink of asking a bliss conscious question, nothing inspiring springs to mind? Fortunately, there are abundant other untold introductory options. For instance, adding uplifting nicknames to the beginnings, bellies, or endings of greetings also kindles mirth.

Do faces brighten whenever you exclaim, for instance, "Good Morning *Sunbeam!*", with heartfelt enthusiasm? Concoctions of exuberant endearments are as infinite as the imagination. So, Wizard of Bliss, let your inborn creative genius loose!

For example,

Hello Treasure Trove.

Greetings Goddess.

Good Evening, Thunderbolt.

Marvelous Moment, Exquisite Embodiment of Divine Perfection.

Hi Angel, what's the bliss?

☼

☼

☼

☼

☼

We evolve as our language evolves.

Co-Creating Beautiful People

Everyday conversations can be fairytales if one enjoys waltzing with words. Our Blissful Lips can paint luscious terms of endearment for reminding everyone how special we all are and how wonderful we can be. Uplifting epithets pose friendly means for joyously addressing whomever we encounter. Let us declare our most playful perceptions of the precious human gifts before us.

By being outrageously ecstatic and absurdly friendly, we invite people to do the same. Joyous enthusiasm is irresistible, especially when personalized. We can concoct cheerful epithets for addressing associates such as "Ecstasy Called Erica", "Joy Called John", or "Miracle Called Mona".

Spontaneously jot down the names of seven special people who feature significantly in your life, then beget an epithet for each.

1.

2.

3.

4.

5.

6.

7.

Spontaneous Introductions

Why do we address our friends with the same old dusty names day after livelong day, when creating intriguing novel names is such fabulous fun? For instance, imagine being at a party where you spontaneously decide to introduce two friends in a new light. What would you call them?

Perhaps you'd like to experiment with what I once said upon realizing that I'd temporarily mentally misplaced the names of two acquaintances from the ancient past. Here's what I said:

It is my profound pleasure to introduce you two. Butterfly, this is Heavenly. Heavenly, meet Butterfly.

After this introduction, 'Heavenly' and 'Butterfly' were delighted, at ease, and smiling since most everyone enjoys an unusual compliment.

When spontaneously introducing people to each other, the more ecstatic and beautiful, the better. The more outrageously, creatively positive our terms of endearment, the more broadly everyone will grin.

How would you creatively introduce people?

☼

☼

☼

Let's legalise happiness.

Who Are You?

Who *are we*, aside from our parentally given names?

> *Who am I? I'm Heavenly and this is Butterfly.*
>
> *Bliss is my true nature. And yours?*
>
> *I'm astonishingly free, just like you.*
>
> *An embodiment of celebration, thanks be to you.*
>
> *We are mysteries even to ourselves. Wonderful, isn't it?*
>
> *I'm one of the people of the sun. And you?*

When asked "Who are you?" instead of automatically answering with the name your parents chose to name you, how would *you* greet the opportunity creatively?

☼ I am a person of Heavenly Harp music

☼ I am one of God's beloved children

☼ a messenger of God

☼

☼

Refreshing approaches evoke playful responses.

Where *Are* We From? The Rare And Flagrant Truth

Nothing inspires us as much as the rare and flagrant truth. Speech that is liberated from predictable responses perks our ears and opens us to possibilities.

Many modern societies define strict parameters as how to answer the question "Where are you from?" It can be surprising to learn that the dictates of civilization require a pre-packaged political answer to this question as demonstrated by the following conversation:

I'm from Auckland. Where are you from?

Would you like to know the true or the politically correct answer?

I'd like to hear the truth, of course.

Then, I'm from the ethereal field from which all life is manifest.

What?

The truth is, I come from the etheric field, the substratum of reality.

I mean, where are you *really* from?

Just like you I come from ether, wind, water, fire, sun, sky and earth, which comprise us and continuously stream through us.

What I meant to ask is, where were you born?

Do you mean geographically where did my mother happen to be when this body left my mother's womb hundreds of moons ago?

Yes, yes, precisely.

Geographically this body was born on top of a swamp at the lip of a vast plain.

You're not going to tell me where you're from, are you?

Do you mean politically? As in which city or state?

Yes, that's what I want to know!

Why in heaven would you like to know that? Cities, states and countries are political entities. We've just met. Would you really like to relegate our conversation to the realm of politics? Where do we really come from? Where were we before we were conceived? Now that's intriguing!

Where Did You Say You're From? I Mean, *Originally*?

In other words, where were you prior to your conception?

☼

What did you look like before your parents were born?

☼

Where were you prior to the birth of Earth? What were your genes up to millions of years ago?

☼

Since the precise date of the origin of humanity and remains a fantastic mystery, one of the most honest answers is, "I do not know." Here follow a few other options worthy of consideration:

Where am I from? How profound. Do you enjoy philosophy?
I'm from a place of joy and freedom.
Some of the relations claim that we're from Gondwanaland.
We are born of stars and darkness.
I hail from a proud and ancient lineage of sperms and eggs.
It's a mystery. No one knows. Isn't it marvelous?

When asked where you are from, does your response liberate and generate joy? What are the most luminous truths of your origin? Where *are* you from?

☼

Where are you based?	*I'm body based. And you?*
Where is your home?	*My home is in my heart.*
How can I get a hold of you?	*Open your arms.*
Where are you living?	*I'm living and I'm here;*
	thus, I'm living here.

How Old *Are* You?

Fortunately, no law requires us to reduce the expanse of our magnificent life journey to a number. We are more than numerals. We are magnificent works of art in progress, fabulously ancient yet ever new.

Considering this, saying "I am 24" or "47" or even "not a day over 129 years young" seems potentially misleading, if not absurd. Hooray, Intriguing Eternal Enigma You, for the freedom of choosing to honour the mystery of your time-transcendent existence by playfully responding to the question "How old are you?"

I'm average for my age.

How old is the wind which whispers our antiquity? How old are the elements, which continuously swish and swirl through us?

Beginningless, endless, timeless and; therefore, ageless.

How old are you?

☼

☼

☼

We don't stop playing when we grow old;
we grow old when we stop playing.

Finis

Creating The Best of Times

Have you ever wondered why you wonder what time it is? Do you ever transcend the urge to consult your watch when asked?

The common question "What time is it?" offers frequent opportunities for us to express exactly what we would like to experience at any given moment. With a bit of blissful contemplation, answering this query can evoke unexpected happiness.

Do you have the time?
Yes I do. And plenty of it.

What time *is* it?
That's a marvelous question!
It's time for a song./ It's time for a hug./ It's time for celebration.

☼

☼

What time *is* it?
What a delightful question!
It's time to gaze./ It's time to dance./ It's time for appreciation.

☼

☼

Wherever we go, it's essential to make good timing,
with the emphasis on good.

Ken Pirsig

Initial Blissful Courtesies

The origin of a smile is usually another smile.

Amidst the bustle of modern life, initial blissful courtesies are occasionally forgotten. Fortunately, there is an easy antidote to those moments of conversational alienation, a very simple way to restore friendliness and human dignity. It is this: before asking for anything from anyone, be friendly first - no matter how inwardly focused or rushed you may choose to be.

Creating pleasant moments of sharing and caring in every conversation heightens our life experience immeasurably, even when simply asking for directions, as illustrated here:

Glorious day, is it not? Exceptionally splendid morning to you! How are you on this marvelous Monday morning? (And if all is well) Glad to hear it. I'm feeling rather fabulous myself. Considering that I'm lost. Would you be so generous as to tell me the way to…? Thank you. May you enjoy the day to the utmost.

When you ask for directions, what do *you* say to add to someone's happiness?

☼

Life is so precious that we must proceed slowly,
so as not to miss any of it.

Thai proverb

Empowering Dreams

With the ease of a breeze we can foster our loved ones' dreams by bestowing mere morsels of encouragement. For example, to a friend who is convalescing, one could exclaim "Hello Energy Temple of Supernatural Health", to an aspiring artist "Hi Conduit of Creativity", to a budding musician "Good Morning Marvelous Musician", and to your beloved "Good Evening Pulsar of Perpetual Lovingkindness".

What could you nickname your seven closest kith and kin to empower them to pursue their dreams?

1.

2.

3.

4.

5.

6.

7.

Experiment with complimenting your intimate relations, even if it startles them at first. Eventually expand the horizons of your heart to beam the dreams of all.

Your Destiny Is In This Word

Have you ever considered which one word has the most impact on a person's life? The word of singular influence is the birth mantra, commonly known as the given name. What is the meaning of your decidedly important first name?

☼

What were the original meanings of your middle and surnames? (If you don't know, please do find out!)

☼

☼

Do these meanings powerfully express your highest truths?

☼

How did your parents or you choose your first name?

☼

Do you enjoy your name's melody of sounds?

☼

How do you feel in relationship to the name you use when you introduce yourself?

☼

Due to a name's far-reaching significance, naming a child used to be a sacred rite, which often entailed praying, fasting, and consulting an oracle, elders, signs, and even one's own dreams, all the while observing the child, whether born, or yet-to-be-born, with reverence.

Have you observed how the ancient meanings of names influence people's chosen life paths? What impact does your name have on you?

☼

Self-Entitlement Experiments

While traveling exuberantly one month, I decided to don a new name each morning. This is relatively easy to do when walking through the alps, therefore, journeying daily to a new location. I'd often arrive somewhere at twilight, thrilled to bed down on a patch of pebbles beneath the stars. Each dawn, as the first morning rays revealed the new surroundings, I would spontaneously choose a new name.

Surprisingly, several of 'my' names such as Miraculous, Free, Snow, Glad-To-Be-With-You, Spontaneous, Audacious, Iluvu, Solar Blossom, Absolutely, Here, Smiling Heart, Sunbeam, Photon, Proton, Quiet, Quintessence, and Alleluia produced such fascinating experiences, elicited such intriguing responses, and felt so satisfying that by evening I would wish the day would endure forever! On some days songlike names, succulent to the ears, of unknown origins and never written, would be chosen such as Hiyatahay, Malamalah and Zubaluwubalu. Consistently calling oneself by a new name throughout the day is a blissipline that arouses profound shifts in consciousness.

Names are incantations. While a carelessly chosen name can harm, a carefully chosen name can heal, liberate and empower a person. Savvy anthropologists know that those tribes renowned for their unusual joyfulness traditionally choose names rich with meaning.

If you were to change your name, what would you choose to call yourself today? How about tomorrow? What do you love? Which words embody your essence? What is important, true, beautiful... *you*?

Reverently, yet playfully, may you give tribute to your self by choosing oodles of new names, while remembering that names are self-fulfilling prophecies:

☼   ☼

☼   ☼

☼   ☼

Bestowing Gifts of Cherished Words

Here's an easy means by which to offer everyone the rare, exquisite pleasure of uttering their favourite words.

> 'What's your name?' he enquired.
> 'What's your favourite word?' she asked.
> 'Splendiferous' he said.
> 'Amazing' she declared. 'My name is Splendiferous.'

Which words do your loved ones especially cherish? (If you've never asked, you may be delightfully surprised.)

For added happiness, offer your loved ones the option of calling you by their favourite words or visa versa.

Not so long ago, naming was frequent, fluid and fantastically fun. Today's naming rites are often diametrically opposed to those of our prehistoric ancestors. In the past, when something significant arose during the course of two people's communing, they may have offered each other new names.

People also renamed themselves when they stepped into life anew by embracing an expanded understanding, a fresh identity, a mastery of skill, or an appealing sound vibration. Consequently, most everyone enjoyed several names. Often people were addressed by as many names as the number of people they knew. Imagine that.

What Do You (*Love To*) Do?

You will likely be asked "What do you do?" on hundreds of occasions in the course of a single lifetime. Thus the question "What do you do?" offers hundreds of opportunities for uplifting conversations while inspiring everyone you encounter, including yourself.

If you could do anything, what would you do?

☼

☼

☼

Which actions generate the most joy for you?

☼

☼

☼

What do *I* do?

    (At the moment) I appreciate, celebrate and co-create.

When asked "What do you do?" I mentally translate the question into "What do I (*love to*) do?"

And you? What do *you* (*love to*) do?

☼

☼

☼

The Gracious Would Say Would

According to unabridged dictionaries, the original root of the word 'want' conveys *lack and desperation*. These meanings are less than entirely bliss conscious. Oh, what to do?

Fortunately, it's facile to formulate uplifting alternatives to the seventh most commonly asked question in the English language "What do you want to do?" by replacing it with, for example, *"What would you like to do?"* or *"What shall we do?"*

Appetizing options could include:

What would you like to co-create?

How shall we celebrate this occasion?

For heaven's sake (said sincerely!), what could we do now?

In which situations could *want* be transmuted into *would, could, shall* or something joyous else?

☼

☼

☼

May your every word shine forth.

Choice Opportunities

I often feel so exquisitely content that life's mundane details seem unimportant. If, when in a blissful state, I am asked "What would you like to do?" I have carelessly said "I don't care". However, saying "I don't care" may be misleading since we *do* care, of course, even when we choose to focus our attention on some details more than on others.

To ascertain that a carefree attitude not be misconstrued as apathy on these occasions, we can rejoice in our carefree feelings by giving our loved ones these opportunities to decide.

When asked "What would you like to do?" instead of saying "I don't care" how could we more joyously and generously respond?

I am so content. I'd love it if you would choose.

Your choice, Gorgeous. I'll be happy with whatever you decide.

As you like, Precious. Surprise me!

☼

☼

☼

Splendid Suggestions

How can we habitually encourage the sharing of creative ideas while overcoming any habitual resistance to suggestions?

By agreeing enthusiastically!

What would *you* say to express enthusiasm for others' new ideas?

What a marvelous idea!   ☼

Brilliant!   ☼

Fabulous. Let's!   ☼

Let's Be Zany!

Most everyone loves a spontaneous idea bestowed with zest. Instead of asking others "What would you like to do?" we can brainstorm about tantalizing activities now to draw from during possible droughty moments ahead. How often do you surprise your loved ones? How did you last surprise them? How would you like to surprise them next?

☼

If you ever feel stumped, you are welcome to borrow any of these activities culled from my past. That's what friends are for.

☺ *Let's snorkel naked in the dark. Let's secretly fill people's shoes with flowers. Let's sing our conversations out to strangers. Let's get chummy with an insect. Let's give away haikus at bus stops. Let's crawl everywhere for the rest of today. Let's dance our deepest meanings. Let's love vibe everyone we see. Let's hum consciously in harmony and record it for posterity. Let's wander. Let's create a smorgasbord where everything intriguing but food and drink is served. Let's pin up poetry in public places. Let's feast and feed each other. Let's swap outfits, names and personalities. Let's draw hints and paint glimpses of invisible worlds. Let's picket to legalise happiness with smiley signs. Let's re-invent ancient ways of being. Let's originate, explore and consecrate. How free and zany can we be?* ☺

How to generate fabulous future possibilities? Without limitation, imagine, what would you and your family or friends especially enjoy?

Let's...

Let's...

Let's...

These Precious Days

How do you honour happiness in your day-to-day life?

Daily we do lorryloads of activities from flossing our teeth to feeding our feathered friends. Let's take an intimate look at these priorities.

In the left column below list the estimated times you spend doing your twenty most common activities, those that represent the great bulk of how you live your precious life.

Begin with the activities which you spend the most time doing. The first activity will probably be either sleeping or your J.O.B, your Joy Of Being.

Hours/Minutes Daily   Name of Activity

1. _____   _____

2. _____   _____

3. _____   _____

4. _____   _____

5. _____   _____

6. _____   _____

7. _____   _____

8. _____   _____

9. _____   _____

10. _____   _____

11. _____   _____

12. _____   _____

13. _____   _____

14. _____   _____

15. _____   _____

16. _____   _____

17. _____   _____

18. _____   _____

19. _____   _____

20. _____   _____

Total (   )

Did you include all twenty activities? Once you do, be sure that they total 24 hours. Let's look lovingly at what you've written, at how you choose to live your days and nights. What do you value? What does your life reveal about your life?

Which portions of your lifestyle express your most cherished values?

According to activities *not* included, what *don't* you value?

☼

Assuming your ideal lifestyle is already coming true, how would you like to divide the remainder of your precious days? What would you enjoy doing or being more often?

☼

What would you prefer to minimize or delete?

☼

Which others would you like to maximize or add?

☼

Returning to these twenty activities, feel free to make notes beside them to clarify how you would ideally like to spend your days. Modify the hours accordingly so that they still total twenty-four.

Which other choices could you make to narrow any disparities between your current lifestyle and ideal lifestyle?

☼

Don't tell me what you believe. Tell me what you do twenty-four hours a day, and I'll tell you what you believe.

Jerry Ruben

Complimenting The Complimenters

Do you receive compliments exuberantly?

☼

Are you a joy to compliment? Why and why not?

☼

It's a blissful blast to reflect the kind and generous words back to those who compliment us, instead of predictably absorbing them. For instance, when someone offers praise, blissologists often boomerang praise back in various ways.

Thanks be to you! How generous of you. You have a beautiful heart.
How loving. What a thoughtful observation. Such enthusiasm.
You inspire me to do my best to live up to your perceptions.

☼

☼

☼

The art of receiving praise graciously
is an awe-inspiring rarity.

I enjoy affectionately complimenting critics, too. Thanking critics disarms us all, fosters peace and preserves everyone's dignity. Whether we feel that the criticism rings true or not, we can feel grateful that it provides food for reflection. Who knows? The introspection consequent to criticism may result in spontaneous singing ecstasy, brilliantine epiphanies, cascades of laughter, tendermost tears, liberation, celebration and momentous leaps of understanding.

The Universe Is Deaf To Negatives

The universe is deaf to negatives. This means that the cosmic brain is unable to hear negative words such as *not* and *never*. Therefore, when "I am not…" is said, the universe hears "I am…"

Thus, describing yourself as *not, no* or *never* focuses your thoughts upon exactly what you do *not* wish for. Instead of repeating what you would rather *not* wish to experience, boldly state your aims by positively proclaiming only that which you would like to welcome into your life.

The universe loves a void, and loves for each of us to fill it. Whatever we intensely focus on, we will eventually experience. Consistently positive speech creates astoundingly positive circumstances. Which special circumstance would you like to manifest?

☼

Which habit would you like to transcend, and which replacement activity would you ideally prefer to fill the void?
I'd prefer to…

How would *you* positively transmute the phrases on the left?
I don't like…   *I enjoy…*

☼

Don't fall and hurt yourself.   *Kindly proceed with care.*

☼

No worries. It's not a problem.   *It's pure pleasure.*

☼

It's no trouble at all.   *It's a joy.*

☼

I'll never forget this.   *I'll always remember this.*

☼

Conversational Alchemy

The words *don't, won't, can't, haven't, hasn't, aren't* and *isn't* are verbal depressants which enfeeble the life force and dissipate dreams. How would you positively transform, then cheerfully express, the common complaints featured on the left?

What's wrong?   *What's happening?*
☼

Are you ill?   *How are you feeling?*
☼

I don't want to get sick.   *I aim to be healthier than ever.*
☼

You're not listening.   *We can be excellent listeners.*
☼

Don't worry.   *Have faith.*
☼

Don't shout.   *Shall we whisper? Wonderful!*
☼

I won't…   *I would rather…*
☼

I don't want to…   *I'd love to…*
☼

I hate*…   *I appreciate…*
☼

* It's a beginner's blissipline to wholeheartedly renounce this harmful word.

Broadcast Wonderful Habits

Not so long ago, while traveling the world at such a pace that resulted in passing every evening in a new home, I decided for purposes of superb health and happiness, to take up the practice of sleeping al fresco.

Wherever I would sleep the night, upon arrival I would inform the hosts of this "*peculiar* habit of sleeping outside". Consequently, dozens of accommodating friends, half-heartedly yet graciously, offered their back gardens, front lawns, porches, gazebos, tree houses and verandahs - as if I were the most peculiar person with the most peculiar habit.

One evening, upon approaching another friend's home, it dawned on me that instead of awkwardly explaining that "I have a *peculiar* habit", a blissologist would enthusiastically announce, "I have a *wonderful* habit. I always sleep al fresco!"

From that moment forward, to my amazement, whenever I slumber al fresco, by the second cloudless night, the hostess and host eagerly request to join me in sleeping outside. Upon returning to my then home this *wonderful* habit became so infectious that everyone decided to sleep outside with the effect that the bedrooms were left empty at night while the decks were filled with contented stargazers. We subsequently built more decks and roofless cliff dwellings to accommodate us all.

As this example shows, by modifying a single word we can enhance the quality of innumerable lives. In the author's case, the consequences of simply changing the word *peculiar* to *wonderful,* give testimony to the powerful effects of positive speech.

Which of your habits, pastimes and ideas could you re-present as being splendid habits, fabulous pastimes or marvelous ideas?

☼

☼

☼

The Shortest Mantra Is Yes

When answering the telephone, instead of saying "Hello", have you ever tried exclaiming *"Yes! Yes! Yes!"*? Try it at the next phone jingling opportunity. How do recipients respond on the other end?

☼

Yes can heal and manifest. Yes is an actualizing word. To enjoy the many benefits of hearing yes often, consciously frame questions which encourage others to say yes to you. It's a blithe blissipline to refrain from asking queries that require "no" responses. For example, "Do you mind if I...?" is a negative question because to answer it positively requires saying *"No,* I *don't* mind". This question also assumes botheration. In contrast, the open-ended query "How would you feel if I...?" offers an infinite spectrum of uplifting responses to choose from.

Likewise, asking "Are you okay?" suggests that someone is either okay or less than okay. However, she or he may be feeling exceptionally sublime. "Are you okay?" requires a yes or no answer. Meanwhile, asking "How are you?" opens up a rainbow of expressive options. Instead of asking controlling no or yes, black and white queries, we can ask full-spectrum questions that stimulate creative spontaneous responses. How would *you* blissify the queries on the *left*?

Do you mind if I...?   *How would you feel if I...?*

☼

Would it bother you if I...?   *I'd love to...*

☼

Is it a problem if I...?   *Would it be agreeable to you if I...?*

☼

Are you okay?   *How are you?*

☼

One Admirable Virtue

Which seven people feature most frequently in your daily life, and among your seven closest associates, which qualities do you most admire?

Friends   and   Virtues

1. _____   _____

2. _____   _____

3. _____   _____

4. _____   _____

5. _____   _____

6. _____   _____

7. _____   _____

To watch associates blossom,
focus on their virtues.

Positive Perceptions

What are your perceptions about life? How uplifting are your basic beliefs? Complete these sentences by spontaneously sharing your most celebrated views of life by jotting down whatever inspirations spring to heart and mind.

I am…

Life is…

The focus of my enthusiasm is…

The human mind is…

My mind is…

The human body is…

My body is…

Work is…

My work is…

The older I grow, the…

Families are…

My family is…

Friends are…

My friends…

My heart is…

Relationships are…

My most intimate relationship is…

A home is…

My home is…

Traveling is…

My loftiest dream is…

My deepest concern is…

I am most grateful for…

Nature is...

Music is…

Art is…

Science is…

Genius Is…

Communication is…

Spirituality is…

My most significant interest is…

My lifestyle is…

Humanity is…

New Zealand is…

The planet Earth is…

The universe is…

Being alive is…

Freedom is…

Happiness is…

Health is…

Success is…

Peace is…

War is…

Money is…

Love is…

Harmony is...

Singing is…

Wealth is…

Poverty is…

My creative expression is…

My greatest asset is…

My highest spiritual truth is…

My mission is…

This moment is …

My life is…

The future is…

My favourite philosophical phrase is…

Reviewing these core perceptions, how would you describe your general outlook on life?

☼

Do these basic views reflect your highest truths, catalyse the manifestation of your dreams, and enhance the lives of listeners?

☼

☼

☼

Words are meant to be soothing balms and cheerful first aid miracles for the heart, especially during challenging moments. If any of the above perceptions could be expressed even more joyously, play with them until merely reading them inspires you.

From Gloomy Doom To Blissful Bloom

When shadowy bubbles of life arise, blissologists avert any temptation to overstate the negative by claiming it as a gloomy truism for the entire world. Broad pronouncements such as "You can't win", "Life is suffering", "I hate rain", and "Technology is a nuisance" amplify individual incidents, thereby needlessly projecting an exaggerated sense of hopelessness.

May you enjoy transmuting these gloomy pronouncements of doom into wild celebrations that bloom.

You can't win. *The adventure continues.*

☼

Life is suffering. *Life is so precious, brimming with gifts.*

☼

I hate rain. *Rain is beautiful. Rain is life. I love rain!*

☼

Technology is a nuisance. *Technology is modern magic. We call upon the spirit of this equipment to let us know how to proceed. We appeal to our innate genius to clarify this situation.*

☼

Take little note of inconveniences and
make mountains out of every iota of good.

Empathetic Joy

We are all related and ultimately entirely one. Your joy is my joy and my joy is yours. "This is obvious," you who are me may be thinking while reading this, which was written by you over here. Once we experientially realise our essential unity, jealousy effortlessly fades away and empathy arises naturally, thereby allowing us to feel tremendous joy in others' joy.

Uttering "I feel jealous" or "I envy you", even in jest, rapidly dilapidates a conversation. What can be said to transmute our own momentary feelings of envy into empathetic joy?

I envy you.   *Your happiness is my happiness.*

☼

I feel jealous.   *Congratulations. Let's celebrate.*

☼

If someone says "I'm jealous of you", how can we joyfully answer?

> *You're not jealous of me, you're happy for me.*
> *And I'm happy for you too!*

☼

A Correlation Between Love and Encouragement

The greater our love, the more encouraging is our speech. This is particularly evident in moments of woe. How to respond when someone feeling crestfallen approaches us? When a forlorn friend glumly mumbles, "I can't bear to go on", what verbal gifts can we offer?
How about,

Isn't it fantastic that all situations are impermanent?

Shall we explore some possibilities, O Super Luminous Human Beam?

Or,

☼

Gladitude

I freely acknowledge the abundant gifts which life affords.

Stating what we appreciate expands our capacity to give and receive. When we cultivate the blissipline of focusing on the marvels of this moment and proclaiming only positive visions, friends and family come to smile upon seeing us in glad expectation of our overwhelming gratitude.

What are a few of the myriad blissings which you are receiving in this amazing – when you think about it –moment?

☼

☼

☼

☼

☼

☼

☼

☼

(Of course, this list is infinite when we present the present with our presence.)

Compassion Empowers

What specifically distinguishes pity from compassion? Pity weakens, whereas compassion empowers. Pity suggests, "I'm sorry. That is dreadful what happened to you". Consequently, the listener feels sorrowfully dreadful. Compassion, in contrast, calmly affirms, "Look for the good in this situation. Tap your infinite strength. One can never have too much faith. This could be a great opportunity in the making."

What could you say and write that would empower friends and family to meet their current challenges?

☼

☼

☼

What could you write and say to encourage your self today?

☼

☼

☼

May we constantly create imagery
that enables evolution.

Feeling Fortunate And Free Of Complaints

Associating with exceptionally fortunate people, whose lives flow positively and harmonically, can be intriguing. Deeply fortunate people exude a particular magnetic charm, and show how good fortune is created with focused, uplifting thoughts, including amplified gratitude.

The interior activities of relaxing, communing with one's highest source, and visualizing the best possible outcomes for each situation accentuate and improve upon one's good fortune. Good luck is habitual and relative, as well as open to interpretation, as is its opposite.

Happiness is here for everyone. Perhaps surprisingly, however, not everyone is here for happiness. It is a curious fact that some people are not truly happy unless they are perfectly miserable. And you? Do you entertain any cherished complaints or fanciful woes?

☼

If so, what are the outcomes of vociferating these sorrows?

☼

I met once two whining, old people in their thirties, whose miserable lives mirrored their mantra that, "life is a series of problems." Fortunately, everything is as awful or as *awe full* as one's opinion declares it to be.

How can we transmute 'problems' into *life-enhancing joys*? Could such *opportunities* be *adventures*, *challenges* or *light-paths to new connections*? How else could problems be positively described?

☼   ☼

Would you like to free your self of complaints? Is this possible? Absolutely! Complaining is habitual. Being free of complaints is easy.
Simply,

1. Stop Complaining.
2. Start Appreciating.

On Being Problem Free

It's important to understand that saying "It's a problem" creates more 'problems' by giving power to problem consciousness. Claiming to possess a "problem" compounds negative aspects of a situation by needlessly arousing emotions associated with negative beliefs. In contrast, interpreting experiences positively magnetizes situational bliss. If someone says, "I have a problem", one uplifting honest response could be,

"You choose to perceive this situation as a problem at this moment. However, there are infinite ways to interpret it".

How would you respond?

☼

Challenging situations can also be inherently:

illuminating
remarkable
curious
educative
hilarious

☼

☼

☼

If I am for myself alone, what am I?
If not me, who? If not now, when?

The Talmud

Conversational Terrorism

We all entertain likes and dislikes. It's how lovingly we describe our dislikes that influences the quality of our lives. Casually stating that something is terrible or horrible adds terror and horror to the world. Are you occasionally a verbal terrorist or horriblist?

Impulsively blurting out negative statements needlessly broadcasts fear, irritation, frustration and other despairing styles of dis-ease. Shout out only optimistic, life-enhancing words such as "Good heavens!" or:

☼

If some less-than-excellent situation is commonly known, do you have the fortitude to refrain from claiming it to be awful, terrible, horrible, despicable, loathsome, dreadful, tragic, pitiful, shocking, yucky, abhorrent, abominable, outrageous, odious or unbelievably bad? Usually a person inversely complains out of care. If caring is the case, let us say so positively. Caring can also be emitted in silence while conjuring up solutions and encouraging messages to share.

What are some heartening alternatives for "That's terrible"?

Shall we take a moment to infuse this situation with love?
Perhaps this could be perceived as wonderful because…
Something fabulous will grow out of this.

☼

☼

☼

When you speak, your mind is on parade.
Sai Baba

Dashing From Dislikes To Delights

Consider briefly two aspects of living of which you are less-than-enthusiastically-fond.

1.

2.

Which *feelings* do each of these thoughts elicit?

1.

2.

Keeping these in mind, share what you would prefer, enjoy, relish, cherish, admire, celebrate or love. Emphasizing preferences shifts the focus from litanies of dislikes to inspiring delights.

1.

2.

How do you *feel* when imagining each of these?

1.

2.

Whatsoever we seek, we find.
So may we seek with care.

The L Word Is The Cosmic Generator

The L Word is the cosmic generator of joy and conversational magic. Though curiously forbidden or overlooked by some, the L Word is the substratum of existence, though ironically, also what this world needs most. For example, imagine how the world would be if every cabinet, congress, parliament, prime minister and president were to make love-based decisions.

What *is* love? Perhaps *pure intention coupled with capability to relieve suffering and offer joy*. Certainly, love elicits multitudinous definitions. How would *you* define love?

☼

Gladly exclaiming what we love with enthusiastic fervor delights and ignites hearts and dreams. Watch how conversations take flight when you simply voice a few facets of whatever you love about life, such as:

I love…

I love…

Which love stories, love songs and/or love quotes do you especially enjoy sharing during conversations?

☼

☼

Attention Activists

Join in with thousands of other blissologists who are visually broadcasting uplifting parables, lovacious quotations, empowering paintings and poetic inspirations on public notice boards, websites, refrigerators and other prominent places.

Lovely Mathematics:
Universal Formulas For Realizing Unity

Lovely Mathematics is unique in that the answer to every equation is already answered. Lovely Mathematics has cracked the riddle of the universe. While other mathematics focus on finding the solution to suit equations, Lovely Mathematics aims to find equations to suit the solution. Since the solution has already been found, the rest is play, and this is precisely how the universe works.

Assuming the universal nature of the universe, how can love be expressed in equations?

1) lovely $\dfrac{us}{he \times she}$ = oodles of us = 1 we = 1 lovely

2) 1 lovely gazing you + 1 lovely grinning me = 1 lovely we = 1 lovely

3) lovely $\dfrac{us(you + me + she + he + they + we)}{me}$ = $\dfrac{we}{me}$ = we = 1 lovely

4) *If* 7,000,000 humans = 1 humanity = 1 lovely
   and 23 billion known species = loveliness
   then, earthlings = 1 lovely x loveliness = 1 lovely

Even for those once erringly considered to be not-so-mathematically-inclined, exquisite equations are now being discovered which are shedding new light on old love conundrums. How would you express your relationships mathematically? Geometrically?

☼

☼

☼

(Lovely Mathematics for couples counseling is being developed internationally.)

I - Free Conversations

A little less me, a little more we, elicits a sense of unity.

The words *I*, *me*, *my* and *mine* are the treasures and the trappings of our precious egos. The more *I*, *me*, *my* and *mine* are said, the more we feel separated and alienated by the mental images of separate spheres that the words *I*, *me*, *my* and *mine* create.

Consciously minimizing the use of the word *I* enhances conversational intelligence and intimacy. Likewise, the frequent, unconscious use of *I* creates inverse effects. Succeeding at being conversationally I-free is commendable. Perhaps you already purposely formulate thoughts and sentences so that they are I-free. Let's try speaking I-lessly for the duration of the next conversation now, and see what happens. (If you are alone, consider picking up the phone.) What do you observe?

☼

Anyone can rekindle arcane ways of transmuting the competitive [and exclusive] pronouns *I, me, my, you, they* and *them* into the cooperative [and inclusive] pronouns *we, us, one* and *ours.* Initially this calls forth considerable blissipline. Why can the pervasive English custom of commencing sentences with *I* be so challenging to relinquish?

☼

the island called we-land

forsake that place called me-land
of i, my, mine and sorrow
alight on the i-land of we-land
of us and we and our.
amble the lands of love lexicon
inclusive affectionate fun
where never is heard a separatist word
where speech reigns inclusive, yes, one.

Moving From Me To We

WE and ME are mirror images. ME is WE upside down.

$$\frac{\text{WE}}{\text{ME}}$$

You see, ME is topsy-turvy. Which is rather uncomfortable. While saying ME depresses and distances, saying WE uplifts and unites. How would *you* transmute these ME phrases into WE phrases?

I know.   *We concur.*

☼

I'm hungry.   *Shall we enjoy some sustenance?*

☼

I have an idea.   *Let's.*

☼

When we first speak I-freely, suddenly we see the world differently. We may spontaneously speak less, listen more attentively, and understand more wholistically. Which kinds of themes and messages tend to be dropped in I-free conversations?

☼

Which kinds of themes and messages tend to flourish?

☼

☼

☼

Treasured Tales

Think of a few personal stories that you most often relate. Let one story that you particularly enjoy sharing spring to mind. However, this time, tell it from a third party's perspective, by replacing *I* with *she* or *he*.

☼

Is the story's new version more, less, or equally as enticing, and why?

☼

The story proposes which ideas and arouses which feelings?

☼

What important messages would you like your stories to convey?

☼

Foregoing Futile Elaborations

Blissologists refrain from saying the obvious phrases "In my opinion", "I think" and "I believe" prior to expressing an opinion. These futile filler phrases needlessly dilute and slow the flow of ideas by drawing attention away from the topic of discussion and toward oneself.

Rejoice Rejoice That We Have Choice

As adults we freely choose, whether consciously or unconsciously, how we live every moment of our lives, as we continuously respond to the ceaseless opportunities that life affords.

Freedom is the greatest joy, especially when we are aware of it. At close inspection, freedom is akin to a glistening multi-faceted gem. The many facets of freedom include spiritual, creative, contemplative, linguistic, familial, conversational, geographical, emotional, cultural, physical, financial, social, environmental, ambient, and attitudinal freedom as well as the freedom of how we enjoy time.

It may feel strange and surprising to realise that we are completely free, that we do not have to or need to do or be anything. If the truth be told, we need not be in this life form at all! We do not even have to live.

Wisely we choose life, and with this choice we are free to decide exactly how we respond to life moment after precious moment, whether we opt to choose with lesser or greater awareness. Attentively honouring one's inherent freedom is empowering.

However, caveat emptor, resplendent reader, beware: consciously replacing "I have to" and "I need to" with "*I'd like to*" and "*I'd love to*" may result in sudden rushes of inexplicable ecstasy.

It's fun to frequently consider the many benefits of whatever we are doing throughout the day.

For example, I never "have to go to the bank." Instead I say,

"*I'd like to go to the bank.*" (I'm grateful to have money to deposit. Wherever we are headed, if we gratefully consider it, there is a benefit.)

Instead of "I need to go to bed now", try "*I'd love to go to sleep now.*" (because it's a pleasure to go to sleep early feel fresh in the morning).

"I must go." (Must we?) It feels better to say, "*I'd like to go now. It's been a pleasure.*"

We Always Choose What We Do

It can feel deliciously liberating to acknowledge that we do not *have to* fix the car, feed the children, take a shower or tidy the house! We do these because there are associated benefits that we appreciate.

When we think of the benefits of doing what we do, we claim our freedom by consciously choosing what we do and say throughout each day. By claiming our freedom we empower others to do the same. Consider the following perhaps overlooked, habitual activities. What do you appreciate about each of them?

I enjoy washing dishes (if I am fortunate enough to have some) because...

I appreciate preparing dinner (if food is available) because...

I relish a bath (when I am in a place to enjoy one) because...

What do you appreciate about your three most common daily activities?

I am grateful for...   because...

I appreciate...   because...

I celebrate...   because...

We freely choose how much we enjoy each extraordinary ordinary moment of life. Our every activity and conversation is precisely as enjoyable as we decide it is.

Look To This Day

for it is life
the very life of life
in it's brief course
lie all the verities
and realities
of your existence;
the bliss of growth
the glory of action
the splendor of beauty
for yesterday is
already a dream
and tomorrow is
only a vision
but today well-lived
makes every yesterday
a dream of happiness
and every tomorrow
a vision of hope
look well therefore
to this day

Anonymous

Questionable Sunrise Questions

Which questions do you ask yourself as you first awaken to the morning? A survey revealed that the following seven questions comprise those most frequently asked upon coming to 'consciousness'.

1. What time is it?
2. Is it late?
3. What day is it?
4. What do I have to do today?
5. Why did I go to sleep so late last night?
6. Which problems should I try to avoid today?
7. What could go wrong today?

These common queries create a silly sense of panic and hurry just as the first beams of naturally happy tender thoughts could be shining into your mind thereby bringing forth your day. We can wake up joyously each morning. We can wake up consciously and in love with life.

Those who habitually stay awake later than optimum health would suggest can prepare themselves for a dynamic tomorrow by going to sleep before the first yawn. To accomplish this, some people initially set an alarm early in the *evening* to remind them to go to sleep early. By slumbering early, we, of course, naturally wake up early with plenty of time and no need for an alarm clock. Waking to an alarm is an alarming habit that fills the body with fear.

Upon waking, do you give yourself the enjoyment of a few moments delighting in where you are, feeling the comfort of the bed if you have one, of your loved one if there is one, and the relaxed pleasure of a few stretches to extend sublime feelings of bedly contentment into the day?

How do you enjoy commencing the day?

☼

Let The Sun Shine In

Asking conscious sunrise questions awakens wondrous possibilities. These queries are among the author's morning friends. How would *you* answer them? Before you do, if you are not already there, feel free to slink back into bed and luxuriate for optimal ambience.

What are the blessings of the moment?

☼

What are my ideals and how can I live them today?

☼

How can I greet the day in a healthy way?

☼

How can I enhance calmness and deepen peace?

☼

What would Creativity explore?

☼

What is the focus of my enthusiasm?

☼

What are my highest happiest truths? How can I manifest them today?

☼

How can today be absolutely dreamy, and how can I create this?

☼

What would the Universe like me to do today?

☼

Your Seven Sunrise Questions

When you first awaken, which questions do you most often ask yourself?

☼

☼

What kind of internal ambience do these questions create?

☼

☼

Which seven sunrise questions would you ask yourself to consciously invoke a joyous start to the day?

1.

2.

3.

4.

5.

6.

7.

By asking brilliant questions, I illuminate myself.

Consciously Creating Your Inner Ambience

We are what we think.
With our thoughts we create the world.

The Dhammapada

How would you describe the personal inner ambience that you'd like to create in each of these realms of your life?

Spiritually

☼

Mentally

☼

Emotionally

☼

Physically

☼

How and what can we communicate to awaken the best of
everyone we encounter, including ourselves?

Creating The Day

Affirmations are positive statements consciously chosen. Affirmations inspire us to create visions that set the tone for the day ahead. Which affirmations could enhance your life experience? Which of your highest wisest truths would you like to manifest today?

☼

☼

☼

☼

☼

The origin of the word 'affirm' means *to make firm*, as in affirming your wishes. Frequently declaring even generic affirmations, such as "Life is wonderful!" and "We love" can catalyse powerful change.

Which affirmations elicit smiles from your insides?

☼

☼

☼

☼

When we love life unconditionally, life loves us back.

Making Relishing Requests

By emphasizing what we love and proclaiming it, accentuating the positive and exclaiming it, we can smoothly transmute our own complaints into relishing requests.

Commencing requests with "*I love it when...*" cheerfully emphasizes the inspiring side of whatever you would like to request of your loved ones, including your adorable self. Note, for example, the following fundamental shift in perception between these two:

"I'd rather that you *not...*" → "*I love it when you(or we or I)...*"

What would you like to lovingly request in your life?

I love it when...

I love it when...

I love it when...

Inferior Feelings Are Overcome By Stating What We'd Like

Those of us with conversational low self-esteem can alleviate this by speaking up and stating what we'd like, instead of giving away personal power by asking excessive permission from other adults. The examples on the left needlessly disempower the speaker, while those on the right empower healthful confidence.

Can I say something? → *There is something important I'd like to say.*

☼

Can I go to the restroom before you speak? → *One moment please.*

☼

The Spontaneous Glad And Glum List

Understanding what supports our own happiness is a prerequisite for communicating happily. In this blissful light, it is essential to comprehensively consider the effects of the places, people, activities and experiences that comprise our lives.

Without taking into account what you *should* feel, spontaneously scribble down the names of the places, people, activities and experiences that tend to gladden you on the left, and those that tend to render you glum on the right. What are your gut feelings? Stop only when the list is completed. Your answers may be surprising.

The Spontaneous Glad And Glum List

Glad	Glum
☼	☼
☼	☼
☼	☼
☼	☼
☼	☼
☼	☼
☼	☼

Healthy Communication

Do you cherish and respect yourself enough to continuously give yourself optimum health? (If not, how often do you love yourself so?)

☼

When have you felt unusually healthy and happy? Which factors would you attribute to these moments of heightened well-being?

☼

☼

☼

Approximately which percentage of the time do you enjoy radiant health and sublime happiness?

☼   %

What could you do, think, say or be to maximize health and happiness? What healthy habits do you enjoy?

I love feeding birds in bed, wandering barefootedly in cushiony woods, singing to the rising sun, revering and being beneath trees, feasting on the energy within the air, swimming with dolphins, dancing with stars, tides and moon, sharing victuals, vespers and dreams, giving gifts of words and gazes, exploring inner worlds, and thanking, ever thanking.

What are some special loves that optimize your health and happiness?

☼   ☼

☼   ☼

☼   ☼

Universal Affirmations

Blissologists include *everybody* in affirmations. After all, we are all connected, all hanging out on this tender little planet *together*. Your welfare affects my welfare as mine does yours. So, it's natural to expand our vista by wishing for everyone whatever we wish for ourselves. For example, saying "All beings radiate health and happiness" is infinitely more all empowering than, "I radiate health and happiness". What would *you* wish for yourself and everyone in the following areas:

Universal Livelihood Affirmations:

We are discovering our life's purpose.
Our work is inspired and inspiring.
We are manifesting our dreams.

☼

☼

☼

Universal Relationship Affirmations:

May all beings abide in joyous harmony.
May all relationships grow more virtuous each day.
May peace-filled love flow from my heart to your heart and to all hearts in the universe.

☼

☼

☼

Universal Energy Affirmations:

Our bodies are energy temples of supernatural health.
All beings are vibrant conductors of vital electric force.
Limitless and alive, we thrive by freely creating boundless energy

☼

☼

☼

Universal Prosperity Affirmations:

(Did you know that prosperity originally meant 'wellness in all ways'?

The universe is prosperous.
We freely tap into infinite riches within.

☼

☼

Universal Affirmations For Spiritual Well Being:

We are consciousness embodied.
By our inner visions, we proceed.
Everything is so divine.

☼

☼

☼

Declaring Your Day

Those who say, "Have a nice day" are at serious risk of having a nice day themselves. Would you prefer a nice day or would you like to live with a tad more pizzazz?

An intriguing study shows that neglecting to wish people *something uplifting*, has mixed, including negative results.

In contrast, I attribute a portion of my apparently unusual amplitude of joy to the wishes that I wholeheartedly convey to whomever I have the good fortune to encounter. For example,

May this be an auspicious day for you.

May your dreams come true.

Supernatural health to you.

Much magic ahead.

May the bliss be with you.

What would you wish for others that *you* would love to experience?

☼

☼

☼

Declare your day by giving it away.

Welcome Back To Now

Today could be the best day of our lives. Today is the only day we truly have, since the past has left us, and the future has not arrived. So why long for what has happened or get excited over things that are yet to come? May we squeeze the juicy sweetness out of every moment.

Have you noticed how time is intrinsic in us, yet how it mysteriously disappears when we feel fully alive? Habitually dwelling in other time zones often arises from unconscious desires for being elsewhere due to unhappiness with present circumstances. Meanwhile life is happening dynamically here and now, and the bliss goes on.

The blissipline of being present entails devising ways to joyously guide past, future and elsewhere-oriented conversations back to what's happening right here right now. What would *you* say be present?

Welcome back to the present! How shall we celebrate this occasion?

What a privilege it is to be here now.

Listen! Do you hear that? Shall we in the ambience for a moment?

☼

☼

☼

To practice shifting the focus to what's here now, how would you gently guide these future-oriented conversations back to the present?

Do you think all terrestrial life forms will be transplanted due to an alien invasion in the year 2027?

☼

What will you be doing in ten years? *(What will we be doing in 100?)*

☼

74

Thing-Free Conversations And Money-Free Talk

If we are prone to plunging into the quagmires of materialism, the questions "How much does it cost?" and "How much did you pay for it?" may become perilous conversation-fillers.

Inquiring about prices is rarely expansive, though it can be expensive, that is, costly to the quality of your conversations. If you would like to know the price of something, consider experimenting with the blissipline of enquiring directly from the merchant, in lieu of derailing precious conversations. May we liberate ourselves from the pandemic of price-fixation.

Complimenting and honouring the human spirit begets considerably more bliss than complimenting human paraphernalia. For instance, imagine replacing the compliment "What a lovely dress. Where did you get it?" with simply, *"You're beautiful inside and out."*

Think of three common materialistic compliments:

1.

2.

3.

Which related alternative compliments do you imagine could shift the focus from things to beings?

1.

2.

3.

Can we resist habitual urges to discuss how astoundingly little or much we paid for our possessions? Boasting about bargains reduces both our beautiful things and our beautiful selves to pecuniary triviality.

Refraining from discussing prices and things encourages the opening of a universe of fascinating discussions. Which subjects intrigue you that you would prefer to discuss?

☼

☼

☼

☼

☼

Which questions could you ask to guide conversations in the direction of each of the above topics?

☼

☼

☼

☼

☼

Are We Human Havings or Human Beings?

In English it is common, even permissible, to speak about people as if we own them. We've all heard people introduce a spouse by saying "This is *my* wife". However, the same person could just as easily have said, "I am her husband" or "We are rather fond of each other".

Would you say "I would like to *have* a child" or "I would like to *be* a parent"? By emphasizing *being* rather than *having*, we can, as human *beings*, make our sentences more *be*coming.

How would you describe a few special aspects of your life as *being* rather than *having*?

☼

☼

☼

Enjoying Doing

Part of the thrill of being human is our relative mobility compared to trees and shrubs. Doing can be delightful, so emphasizing *doing* rather than *having* gladdens conversations. Would you say, for example, "I *have* a guitar?" or " I *enjoy playing* guitar?" Would you say, "I *have* a garden" or "I *enjoy growing* a garden"? Though the words differ only slightly, the essence and effects of these approaches differ substantially.

How would you describe a few of your central activities as *enjoying doing* rather than as *having*?

☼

☼

☼

Cheerfully Letting Go

Today, saying 'my house' and 'my things' may seem normal since humanity is now largely submersed in a craze of possibly unprecedented materialism. Nonetheless, and all the more, letting go of claiming ownership enables conversations to take flight.

It's easy to lighten conversations by simply replacing 'my' with 'the' as seen in the following example.

My giraffe is in my bath. → *The giraffe is in the bath.*

What are three possessive phrases that *you* commonly say?

1.

2.

3.

How could you transmute each phrase into something more expansive?

1.

2.

3.

Do we own our things, or do 'our' things own us?
Moreover, are we caretakers, or are we being taken care of?

If You Must Boast, Praise Others

Boasting, as marvelous as it may momentarily feel, sometimes saddens listeners, so cannot be recommended. If you are one to habitually promote yourself to others, try boasting about others with equal enthusiastic zeal. Is the heart of self-promotion competitive or positively unifying? What are the causes of boasting?

☼

Living thoroughly in bliss entails relinquishing winning and losing, since happiness at the expense of another's happiness is limited and unsustainable. Blissologists avoid arousing envy by praising.

Exuberantly give generous credit to those who sustain you, including the invisible world, the living earth, and earthlings, complimenting especially whomever has just complimented you.

In which two ways are *you* most frequently praised, and how would you most graciously receive each of these compliments?

☼

☼

A pleasant air can be created by replacing what "I'm good at..." with "I enjoy..." then asking what others enjoy to prevent a personal monologue. What, for example, are your talents and strengths?

I enjoy...   *And you? What do you enjoy?*

I'm fond of...   *Are you? What are you fond of?*

I like to...   *And you?*

Most People or Exceptional People?

Most people talk about how *most people* are not living wisely. It's widely known that most people watch too much television, eat too much, exercise too little, work at uninspiring jobs, live by questionable ethics, and often neglect to manifest their loftiest dreams. So why mention it?

The opportunities are ceaseless for criticizing *most people* who comprise modern humanity at large. However, You With The Blissful Lips Beware: criticism is a form of complaint, so woe be to anyone who entertains such conversations.

Why then is talk of *most people* so prolific? Could complaining about most people serve as a subtle means of increasing one's self-image at the expense of society at large? Could *most people* be used as an excuse for one's own mediocre life? Be forewarned, if we speak of or aim for mediocrity, we will reach it, lest we fall short. However, if we aim for the stars, at the very least we will land in the treetops and enjoy the view.

In lieu of repeating disheartening litanies of how *most people* err, why grumpily complain if we can joyously refrain? Instead, let us focus our verbal offerings on leading the way toward uplifting alternatives and sustainable solutions. What we say about people reveals far more about us. When you talk about people, would you describe your perceptions as more often critical or complimentary, and why?

☼

How much of your conversations do you pass asking about the person with you? How much do you spend asking or talking about those who are elsewhere? Do you tend to talk more about the ways of most people or exceptional people, and why?

*Most people tend to speak of most people whereas
exceptional people tend to speak of exceptional people.*

Exceptional People

To talk of people who live exceptional lives and offer exceptional
solutions, one most likely associates with exceptional people, if not in
person, in books or other media. Who are a few exceptional people
who add inspiration to your life?

☼   ☼

☼   ☼

☼   ☼

Would you include yourself in the list? If you struggled to complete the
list, consider broadening your social horizons and perspectives in
innovative ways.

Geniuses discuss intriguing ideas; intelligent people share useful
information; and mediocre people talk mostly about people, *most
people*.

Radiant Reader, may we bliss consciously relate the brilliant
creations, inventions and virtues of exceptional people such as yourself
who:

> ☼ are lightning streams of positivity
> ☼ celebrate everyone's happiness
> ☼ creatively encourage the realization of dreams
> ☼ enhance others' energy
> ☼ contribute to a wonderful world

Omnipresent Angels

However we relate with the world,
the world reciprocates.

For example, for several winters I dwelt in a forest monastery in tropical Asia. After the first season, I walked out of the monastery without realizing that something interesting had taken place. To my astonishment, the ordinary country shopkeepers and taxi drivers had somehow become enlightened. Moreover, everyone I encountered was suddenly astoundingly friendly, exceedingly generous and deeply kind for no apparent reason. I soon seriously suspected them all to be undercover angels disguised in human suits. Many remarkably blissful days passed before I realised what was going on.

Is it possible to transmute our impressions of those around us by purifying our own perceptions? The evidence is mounting. It is quite possible to view everyone as a precious gift by uplifting our insides and sharing our positive visions of all.

Suggesting, for example, "Hi Conscious Communicator", "I feel honoured to know you", and "You are an angel" can evoke angelic tendencies in both oneself and others.

What would you like to specifically call forth among your closest associates? To accomplish this, how would you address each of them?

☼

☼

☼

☼

☼

Bliss Is Our True Nature

The option to be blissful is omnipresent, because bliss is the undercurrent of creation. Bliss is our true nature, and every other state of being is a rather curious drama. Whatever we embrace, we become. Are there any thoughts that you choose to think or emotions that you choose to feel that delay you from living in continuous bliss? If so, how could you cheerfully redefine these?

☼

Emotions are strongly stirred up feelings. Nobody owns feelings. We simply pick them up, because feelings are not personal, but communal phenomena. Just like picking up a spoon from a communal drawer, you can pick up a feeling, hold on to it, use it, experience it, then, when you are finished, put it back. When we are conscious, we are free to pick up and put down feelings at our discretion. Hence, there is no such thing as "an angry man" or a "fearful woman". The anger does not belong to the man. The man is simply habitually clinging to the 'spoon' of anger, while the woman is gripping the 'spoon' of fear, until they decide to put these down and pick up something else.

We've all grabbed hold of the full spectrum of emotions. How do blissologists let go of the feelings that are useless? When you find yourself in a state of other-than-bliss, what do *you* do that successfully improves your mood?

☼

☼

Which words, lyrics, books or phrases kindle your interior joy?

☼

☼

Sorry Is A Sorry Word

Sorry is a sad word. Sorry is the adjective form of the word sorrow. Therefore, the sad habit of saying "I'm sorry" brings sorrow to conversations. In the interest of bliss, let's minimize from saying this and from doing things that might require it.

"I'm sorry" is considered a necessary polite expression in some English-speaking circles, especially among many British and New Zealanders. Upon approaching someone, well-behaved children are often taught to say, "I'm *sorry*. I hope I'm not *bothering* you." However, this spreads needless sorrow and botheration.

How can one avoid saying "sorry" thereby giving out sorrow without seeming inconsiderate? For example, how would you approach the following situation sensitively yet joyfully?

"I'm sorry. I hope I'm not bothering you."

Good afternoon. Glad to see you. Would this be an agreeable time to speak with you?

☼

Why say sorry over trifles? If you are two minutes late, for instance, why automatically apologize? Those two minutes may be passed enjoyably. Most everyone can benefit from the serenity that a few moments of solitude may afford. If we are not habitually late, yet arrive slightly tardy one day, what could we convey instead of greeting our friends with sorrow? For example, "I'm sorry I'm late."

Hooray! Here we are together again. I'm so glad to see you!

☼

On the other hand, if feelings have been hurt, and the hurt can be more deeply healed by swiftly and sincerely saying "I'm sorry", life is too short and far too enjoyable to hesitate. In the wake of any sincere sorrow, may we share post haste all the compassion, peace and gentle joy we can muster.

Celebrating Sorrows

During challenging times of crisis, optimistic joy can save lives. Moreover, cheerful encouraging words can surprise our associates in to elation. How to would *you* offer uplifting humour and encouragement in these situations?

You lost your job?
Congratulations! You're momentarily free. A better job awaits you.

☼

Your mother died?
She's been liberated? Peace and joy be with her. And peace and joy to us in every precious moment remaining in our lives.

☼

Your car was totaled?
And you lived through it! How shall we celebrate our good fortune?

☼

Your spouse just moved out?
What a wonderful opportunity to discover the exquisite riches that only solitary life affords. You will love it.

☼

You're sad?
Tears are drops of love.
I feel grateful to be here with you now in this tender moment.

☼

There exists a strange joy
that abides deep beneath sorrow.

Swearing Is Magical

Since words are manifestations of energy, and energy is indestructible, words are also indestructible. Where does verbal energy go? It invisibly permeates our environment. Let's consider the powerful effects of swearing.

Swearing, in the modern sense of the word, is a form of pollution. Akin to dropping litter, somebody will eventually have to pick it up. Imagine picking up the energy of the word damn, which means *to curse and to condemn to punishment, especially hell.* Swearing is clearly a pernicious past time.

Why, then, do some people swear? Those who habitually swear often lack a lexicon sufficient enough to clearly, cogently and colourfully express themselves. It is a curious fact that some speakers tend to rarely utter the words love, beauty, peace or joy, as if there is a taboo against what is wholesome, though these same speakers may think little of casually cursing. They are likely unaware that to curse means *to cast a spell.*

Spelling anything aloud or especially writing it out gives magical power to it. Such was the original enchanting use of spelling that is taught today in schools. The concept of swearing as an obscenity is a relatively recent fad invented in the 1800's. Even today, twelve of the thirteen definitions reiterate the sacredness of *swearing*:

1. to make a solemn declaration or affirmation by some sacred being or object 2. to bind oneself by oath; to vow 3. to give evidence or to make a statement on oath 5. to declare, affirm, etc,. by swearing by a deity or a sacred object 6. to testify or state on oath 7. to affirm, assert, or say with solemn earnestness 8. to promise on oath; vow 9. to take an oath 10. to bind by an oath 11. to swear by, a. to name a sacred being or object as one's witness or guarantee in swearing b. to have great confidence in 12. swear in, to admit to office or service by administering an oath 13. swear off, to promise to give up (something).

– Websters' Unabridged

Taking Oaths

An oath is a solemn appeal to the universe or to someone revered to witness one's determination to keep a promise.

All of us have sworn off something. What have you sworn off or, better yet, *into* your existence that has improved the quality of your life? Which are the seven most significant oaths, vows or resolutions you have taken? How did each enrich your existence?

1.

2.

3.

4.

5.

6.

7.

What is your oath of the moment? (What would you like to welcome into your existence?)

☼

Inventive Invectives

Swearing is a learned response. In homes in which swearing is nonexistent, people are prone to respond silently and proceed quietly if something perceived as unpleasant occurs. In homes in which swearing is considered acceptable, people often complain loudly about whatsoever they perceive to be negative.

Accordingly, in homes in which swearing is considered unacceptable, people more often enthusiastically exclaim whatsoever they perceive to be positive. What are the conversational tendencies in your home?

☼

People generally love attention. Therefore, it's interesting to note that in swearing homes, where more attention is given to those who communicate negatively, situations are more often interpreted as negative. The more that complaining is considered acceptable, the greater the likelihood for swearing.

When we choose to interpret a situation as less-than-excellent, instead of swearing or otherwise complaining, what blissful words can we exclaim? Here are a few inventive invectives for your enjoyment:

Good Heavens	*Extraordinary*	*Truly*
Preposterous	*Far Out*	*Extraordinary*
Potatoes	*Ooo la la*	*(Silence can be best)*

☼	☼	☼
☼	☼	☼
☼	☼	☼

Euphoric Euphemisms

This is a simple exercise in looking for goodness.

cheap
excellent value

☼

cold (weather or water)
fresh and invigorating

☼

fat
cuddlesome

☼

old
experienced

☼

lazy
a master of relaxation

☼

stupid
somewhat uninformed

☼

urinate
tinkle

☼

used
well-loved

☼

The Ultimate Truth

Once upon a time, an avid seeker wandered the world in search of the ultimate truth. After countless years of arduous travel, the seeker learned of a venerable sage who was reputed to know the ultimate truth.

So the seeker set out to find her. Hearing that the wise one dwelt atop a particular jagged crag, the seeker trudged across vast rocky ranges, then up the said crag, thereupon encountering fierce tempests of the most trying kinds. Alas, after suffering great tribulation, he reached the sage. Gasping for want of oxygen the seeker implored her, "Venerable One, what, pray tell, is the ultimate truth?"

"The ultimate truth?" she giggled gently. "It is simple. It is this: never argue with anyone."

"WHAT!" scowled the seeker in bitter desperation. "I haven't come all this way only to hear THAT. That's not the ultimate truth!' he shouted enraged.

The wise one paused. "You're right," she agreed meekly. "That's not the Ultimate Truth."

How Could Anyone Quibble? It's Such A Silly Word.

Nonetheless, quibbling ranks as the second leading evening past time, after television, in many homes around the world. The golden question is: What is the root of joyous harmony, and how can we nurture it?

☼

Blissfully Listening Together

If you have two ears and only one mouth, and I have two ears and only one mouth, could this mean that we are both meant to spend the remaining third of our time listening to silence together?

May we listen often and audaciously together. May we joyously suggest it to each other.

"Let's listen!"
"Yes, let's do it!"

A wonderful aspect about listening is that we can listen anywhere anytime. We can make listening dates. *"Let's meet in the bath tub at 8 o'clock to listen."* Meeting in unusual places or natural settings specifically to listen can be especially magical.

The most profound listening can occur in the middle of conversations when a person becomes conscious that she or he is listening. When both people are conscious of listening, even as each one speaks, something mystical happens, an intimate link arises, an undercurrent of unsaid love begins to flow...

What are some of your finest listening philosophies, places, fantasies, experiences, and words of advice?

☼

☼

☼

☼

☼

Listening Empathetically

Conscious listening is deep. It is listening with our hearts and cells, listening with naked toes, listening from the navel of the Earth. Listening with quiet depth evokes subtle nuances that are at other times imperceptible. Listening empathically with your full-bodied attention can be a great adventure.

To listen empathetically requires tremendous love and courage. To be empathetic is to fearlessly step in to the feelings of others, whatever they may be. Listening empathetically leads to discovering others' worlds, thereby expanding one's own.

Listening without empathy is not listening, but hearing. If you find yourself saying, "I don't understand your perspective", you have heard, but not fully listened. Listening often requires clarification and reflection. Regardless of our personal views, the outcome of listening is greater understanding.

Do you have prerequisites for listening deeply? If so, what are they?

☼

In which situations do you tend to listen with your entire attention?

☼

In which situations do you tend to only hear?

☼

Why would you prevent yourself from listening deeply? Moreover, how do you to prevent yourself from being able to listen?

☼

What would you do (and refrain from doing) to set the scene for deep empathetic listening?

☼

Moderating The Extremes

Superlatives include *everybody, nobody, always, never, totally, forever, all, none, best, worst, shortest, tallest, biggest and smallest.* Superlatives, unless in jest, can detract from the speaker's credibility since superlatives are defined as 'extreme and excessive exaggerations'. Weaving superlatives into one's speech often creates inaccuracies thereby compromising the truth. For example, if we say, "Everybody always grumbles" does that mean everyone in the universe?

Emotionally-charged speakers may sputter forth superlatives in an attempt to strengthen their arguments. (As for me, I never exaggerate. Not in a million years.) How would you transmute these superlatives into more accurate, moderate, and inspirational sentences?

She's *forever* questioning everything. (Twenty-four hours a day?)
She can be delightfully inquisitive. It's a symptom of intelligence.

☼

You're *always* criticizing me. (Always?)
Thank you for contributing a fresh perspective.

☼

You are *totally* closed-minded. (Without even an open nostril?)
I love that we are both open to learning new perspectives.

☼

How to soften these superlatives? Please feel free to add your ideas.

always	→	*with frequency*	☼
never	→	*on rare occasions*	☼
all	→	*a multitude of*	☼

Brimming With Bliss

Imagine yourself as a glass of contentment. If you were such a glass, how full of energy would you assess yourself to be at this given moment?

☼   %

Operating from what level of energy is adequate for you? Would 70%, 80% or 90% suffice?

☼

This is a place for gentle reflection. How would you assess your current level of satisfaction with each of the following?

Physical well-being

☼   %

Geographical well being

☼   %

Emotional well-being

☼   %

Intellectual well being

☼   %

Spiritual well-being

☼   %

Creativity

☼   %

Loving life

☼   %

Inner peace and calm

☼   %

Am I living by my values?

☼   %

Am I living by my dreams?

☼   %

Being loving, starting with our selves,
is an extraordinary achievement.

Meniscus Meditations

Have you noticed that when a glass of water is filled to the brim, a thin layer of water rests above the rim? Scientists called this the meniscus. The meniscus is that special extra little bit beyond being full that I call "The Hundred And Oneth Percent". *Anything we do or don't do that replenishes our life force is a Meniscus Meditation.*

Like other batteries, the body-spirit requires recharging when low. When feeling depleted, refraining from speaking boosts energy. *Recharging your body batteries to full capacity is possibly the most important requisite for sustainable bliss conscious communication, because without glowing health, the quality of communication can be compromised.* How many miscommunications have resulted from verbally exerting oneself when insufficient energy was available?

To gather my energy I enjoy luxuriating in delicious spells of quiet solitude, honest rest and creative relaxation. In which ways do you gather energy to replenish your self?

☼

By letting your energy gingerly fill to the brim, drops of energy soon spill over the rim as ready gifts to yourself and others. Energy is indestructible, immortal and abundant. Omnipresent energy is being continuously replenished. Mentally and verbally focusing on optimum states of health can magnetize energy and revive your dynamic ecosystem, until it's habitually thriving, as these examples demonstrate:

I'm tired → *I'm feeling sleepy, so am off right now to enjoy a nap.*
I'm sick → *I'm resting, cleansing and on the brink of deep recovery.*

With a wise dream-directed lifestyle, divine nutrition and bliss conscious communication, you can lead yourself into chronic states of supreme well-being.

Ameliorate It

Feeling lousy?
I'm feeling a little less than fabulous.

☼

Our vacation was disastrous.
Our holiday was surprisingly educative.

☼

The meeting was a failure.
The meeting took some interesting turns.

☼

You don't look well. What's wrong?
How are you feeling?

☼

We disagreed.
We are reaching new heights of mutual understanding.

☼

He's stupid.
He's a genius in the making.

☼

It's freezing outside.
Invigorating, isn't it?

☼

Pro-Creative Compliments

When something less-than-exceptionally-clever is said, we can offer alternative approaches that call upon the person's best, such as: *You are brilliant, and I expect nothing less from you.*

☼

When something unkind is said, we can encourage virtues.
Our true nature always shines through. I love you because you are gentle, considerate and kind.

☼

When someone poses limitations, we can suggest broader options.
Possibilities galore abound. Shall we brainstorm?

☼

Let's live in joy
In love
Even when among those who hate.

Let's live in joy
In health
Even when among the ill.

Let's live in joy
In peace
Even when amidst the peaceless.

Let's live in joy
In freedom
Shining radiantly
Wherever we may be.

The Dhammapada

Loving Your Life

Personal stories grant us special opportunities to share. Do your personal stories make for precious gifts? Our stories unveil us. Are yours grateful, humble or forgiving? How do your stories speak of you?

☼

Which stories do you tell that reveal inspiring memories and truths?

☼

☼

What were a few delightful moments of your childhood?

☼

☼

☼

Which loving gestures of your family or friends have especially inspired you?

☼

☼

Where was the cradle of your civilization? Which places, people or experiences sparked your consciousness?

☼

☼

☼

Who have been your most profound influences, and how have they enriched your life?

☼

☼

What do you appreciate about your chosen path?

☼

☼

What has life taught you thus far? If you please, share some central tenets of your own wise observations and realizations here.

☼

Expect The Best

We can create continuously blissful circumstances by envisioning marvelous outcomes. A fine way to predict the future is to create it yourself by carefully entertaining and sharing only your most positive projections. How would you state what you would like to create in the following situations?

I don't think you are going to cooperate.
Thank you in advance for your assistance.

☼

Looks as if we won't be able to agree.
I feel confident that we will reach an agreement.

☼

I think you intend to selfishly consider only your own interests.
Generosity is our true nature, and we both have generous spirits.

☼

You seem bent on destruction.
You are important, and will contribute to the world in wonderful ways.

☼

About which facet of your future are you most enthusiastically concerned?

☼

What could you say to cast a positively-inspired spell upon it?

☼

Future Thoughts

Our dreams and visions are our templates of reality.

What do you imagine will be the five most significant features of your future?

1.

2.

3.

4.

5.

How do you positively envision these features manifesting?

1.

2.

3.

4.

5.

How do I know that I am succeeding at this?
Bliss Conscious Communication transforms the heart.
The tender become more powerful, and the powerful more tender.

Fear Or Faith? You Decide.

*Courtesy of experiences which offered us
wisdom in the past, we are free to choose our ways
ever more wisely now as we continuously stride into the future.*

When speaking of the future, do you speak fearfully or faithfully?

☼

What are the effects of this?

☼

Which factors decide whether you speak ominously or auspiciously?

☼

Faith was originally *fate*, from Fates, the goddess who embodied fidelity, confidence and deep universal understanding. When conversing about the future, what could the sage in us say to transmute fears (both our own and others) into faith?

*There is a cosmic perfection behind life's many dramas.
What can we do today to enhance the lives of tomorrow's earthlings?
We are free to choose wisely now.*

☼

☼

☼

☼

Why complain about what might not even happen?

Contemplative Commemorations

*Those who drink at midnight on New Year's Eve
are drunk for two years, while those who meditate
on New Year's Eve are meditating for two years.*
Ajan Po

How we choose to commence the New Year foretells our year ahead.
What would be the most auspicious means by which you could
commemorate your New Years?

☼

I invite you to celebrate a precious tradition of writing down the
previous year's treasures, lessons and pleasures on your birthdays,
anniversaries and new years. This is a profoundly rewarding way to
deepen one's journey, heighten one's appreciation, and see the bigger
picture. So why wait! Would you venture to share a few of your last
twelve month's autobiographical challenges, accomplishments and
delights?

☼

☼

☼

How would you describe some of the ordinary yet highly-appreciated
good fortunes of your daily life?

☼

☼

☼

What have you discovered this year?

☼

☼

What have you realised?

☼

☼

Who have you become?

☼

☼

How have you become?

☼

☼

If you could, how would you name this past year?

This was the year of...

How would you name this New Year? (*It begins now!*)

This is the year of...

The Appreciation Game

It is a common and thought-provoking fact that the general populace of poorer countries is usually (unless they are torn by war or cataclysm) markedly happier than the populace of the wealthier nations. Why is this? Here follows a true story as to possibly why.

There lives an exceptionally intelligent, though entirely illiterate young family of nine peasant coffee bean pickers, who slumber together on one enormous, rambling bed head-to-toe-to-head-to-toe-to-head-to-toe-to-head-to-toe-to-head. The parents invited the author to live with them in their humble abode (and share their bed!) situated amidst a coffee grove that stretched across the slope of a formidable lava-hissing volcano in the hinterlands of Guatemala. Inside their simple hut of wood and brambles, we have happily passed many nights playing a simple game while huddled around the fire.

The game begins by gathering two handfuls of red coffee beans from a sack. We then commence to take turns sincerely complimenting other players. With every compliment offered, we give away a corresponding bean. The object of the game is to give away all of your beans. Although participants may occasionally talk over each other or shout with zest, the game is played with a cooperative rather than competitive air; so, relaxation, generosity and hilarity prevail. Among the smaller children the game occasionally degrades into choruses of "muchas gracias" (much thanks). The game ends when everyone is laughing and somebody yawns.

Interestingly, I've been invited to play variations of this game with various tribes in several third world countries. *Some people pass feathers, others pebbles, but most important of all is the passing of compliments.* Try it tonight, if you like, with your family and friends. What do you observe?

☼

Original Grins

In wildness is the preservation of the world.

Henry Thoreau

Do you freely share wild and feral truths, bring up the bizarre, mention the unusually beautiful, court curious conundrums, and express the sacred, including what may, at first, seem apparently absurd? Do you relate unusual, uncanny, hilarious and preposterous observations?

☼

Blissologists can be magnets of creativity, purveyors of surreal dreams, proponents of possibilities, lodestars, augurs, catalysts, stirrers, and visionaries.

Would you venture to share a few of your most profoundly original, zany truths, experiences, inventions, facts, theories, perspectives or opinions?

☼

☼

☼

Abundance Abounds

Bespeak abundance boundlessly, be it abundant butterflies, abundant peace, abundant epiphanies or ??? What would *you* like to experience in abundance, and what could you say to attract it?

☼

Claiming Reframing Opportunities

Even potentially unpalatable phrases provide opportunities for us to practice the blissiplines. The denser the communication surrounding us, the greater the potential for growth. When we are conscious, we can reap the joys of communicating as a means for our own personal transformation.

For example, asking someone to speak blissfully could be, circumstances depending, asking a lot. Instead of frequently requesting that your associates reframe their negative phraseology, what could you suggest?

Asking "Could *I* reframe that please?" gives *you* additional occasions to hone *your* talents for reframing.

To gently include others in a co-creative air, blissologists have been heard wondering aloud, "Hmm…Interesting. How could we reframe that?" Most everyone delights in hearing their phraseology stated positively and exuberantly, though few are initially inclined to reframe their ideas themselves.

Which other gentle inspiring approaches would you use to introduce reframing?

☼

How would *you* reframe the following? Sample responses are italicized.

I think your communication style is disagreeable.
I believe what you are saying is that we can relish our rapport.

☼

Why do you have to be so negative?
Are you suggesting that we try this in a more positive light?

☼

Naturally Speaking

Natural metaphors add sparkle to conversations. How would *you* describe these colour images with metaphors from nature?

red lips
raspberry lips

☼

green eyes
emerald eyes

☼

white hair
cloud-coloured hair

☼

blue skies
forget-me-not skies

☼

black fur
night-coloured fur

☼

orange sunrise
nectarine sunrise

☼

Defining Yourself

Words are mighty, magical, prophetic.

However we define ourselves portends who we will become. How do you describe yourself both to others and to yourself?

☼   ☼

☼   ☼

How could you lovingly steer self-deprecations toward emphasizing the positive in conversations? How would you respond, for instance, if someone says "I'm an unskillful communicator"?

Do you mean to say that you would like to communicate even more consciously?

☼

Consider a few aspects of yourself, that you consider to be less-than-excellent that you share with other people. How could you creatively redefine these in a positive, celebratory light?

☼

☼

☼

First access the infinite potential, then speak.

Why Our Addictions Define Our Religions

The word addiction is an etymological conglomeration of *diction* meaning "speech" and *ad* meaning "to". Hence, addictions are what we speak to people about. Contrary to popular understanding, addictions can be positive.

Religion has been interpreted as originally meaning "allegiance again", while the word *allegiance* stems from "loyalty". Our addictions, what we speak to people about, form our religion, that is, our verbal allegiance or "loyalty again".

To what are you loyal again and again? Which themes most often frequent your conversations? What are the subjects of your enthusiasm? Which seven topics and perspectives comprise your primary "addictions"?

1.

2.

3.

4.

5.

6.

7.

These topics and perspectives also represent seven foundational tenets of your 'religion'. Which facets of this unique religion do you value most, and why?

☼

Boomeranging Thanks

Homeless, scruffy recipients often say "Thank you" upon receiving their sundry scoops of food at soup kitchens. At one Alaskan soup kitchen, the kitchen volunteers generally responded to the many 'thank you's with the North American response, "You're welcome".

However, one volunteer was famous for never saying "You're welcome". Instead, while joyously doling out dollops of mashed potatoes, she would exclaim, "Thank *you* for coming!" as if those often despairing, indigent people were royal ambassadors. As you can imagine, this would elicit smiles from everyone.

Likewise, instead of taking credit for small gestures, let us boomerang gratitude back to the grateful.

North Americans are taught that saying "You're welcome" is polite. However, it can be an automatic, conversation-stopping and potentially condescending response. Rather than saying "You're welcome", blissologists prefer to boomerang thanks back to the complimenter. How can we boomerang thanks when someone thanks us for something?

Thank you for...

Thank you. How generous and kind of you.

☼

Thank you for...

Thank you. Your encouragement is appreciated. However, you *are the* one *to be commended for ...*

☼

On the other end of the sphere, we New Zealanders are taught that it is polite to receive compliments in a self-deprecating manner. However, small monologues about how inadequate we are can also be conversation-stopping. May we receive praise and thanks neutrally, with neither pride nor self-deprecation, focusing instead on feeling grateful for any verbal generosities bestowed.

Dife and Leath

*If we view death as the opposite of life, life is
good and death is bad. But death is the opposite of
birth, not of life. Life is good and death is equally good.*
Hinduism

From out of the heart of a dead tree, a sapling shoots up toward the sky.
This intricate relationship between death and birth leads me to wonder,
precisely where does life begin and death end? Could life and death
inseparably together comprise one cooperative, one organism, one great
mysterious dance of death with life? If so, I call this Dife.

Let us share playful portrayals of the great transition with those who
either miss now-invisible loved ones or have ideas of some day dying.

*the moment of body liberation   ecstatic emancipation
the start of heavenly adventure   the state of boundless love*

How would you most delightfully describe death in your own words?

☼

☼

What would you like to be your departing last words? (And what about
your arriving words?)

☼

What would you like said or read at your funeral and inscribed on your
epitaph, should you choose to have one? (It's easier to communicate
this now rather than later.) Separate sheets

☼

Celebrating Silence

noone spoke
the host, the guest
the white chrysanthemums
ryoto

Here are a few be-humbling ponderings about silence.

When words end, deep communication begins.
Pausing enhances perception and deepens connection.
Avoid loose speech and those who entertain it.
Character is what you think when no one else is listening.
Silence is the handiest yet least-employed freedom of speech.
Few people complain that someone is listening too much.
Significant silence begets significant speech.
Which is of greater benefit right now, my words or my silence?
Listening is beautiful.
Love is a confluence of quiet minds.

What are your sagacious observations and feelings about silence?

☼

Better than a thousand useless words,
is one word that brings peace.
The Dhammapada

Celebrating Solitude

Sometimes there is nothing so thrilling as the prospect of a date alone with myself. How unlonely being alone can be! May you frequently dive deeply into silence to behold its many splendours.

as a bee seeks nectar
from all kinds of flowers,
seek teachings everywhere;
like a deer who finds
a quiet place to graze,
seek seclusion to digest
all you have gathered;
like a being
liberated beyond all limits,
go wherever you please;
and live like a lion,
completely free of all fear

Tantra of Z'oquen

What are your thoughts on solitude? What are its special gifts? How do you celebrate solitude?

☼

Within the mind lurks an untold universe
where marvelous discoveries abide.

Slowing Together

When I find someone chattering or bodily racing beyond the speed of light, I often suggest that we *slow* together. *Slowing* is a conscious decision to speak and move each succulent muscle at a significantly slower rate than we normally do. So, we move like clouds, we stretch like well-napped cats and slowly we flow like gracious Tai Chi masters.

S*lowing* heightens awareness, enriches breathing, enhances receptivity, and calms the body, mouth and mind. Soothing yet energizing, *slowing* feels fun. It is helpful to mention how slow to go. For example, you could suggest,

"Let's *slow* to half of our current speed for a little while. Shall we?"

(If you opt to suggest this, do so *slowly*.)

Emphatically Thanking

When saying 'thank you' aloud, which do you emphasize: THANK you, thank YOU, thank you or THANK YOU?

☼

Which variety of 'thank you' likely sounds the most grateful?

☼

Thanking someone without demonstrating enthusiasm with one's voice nullifies the gratitude expressed. I often enjoy speaking slowly and deliberately, letting each leisurely syllable of every eminent word shimmer forth resplendently. Speaking emphatically and enthusiastically arouses sincerity.

Enthusiastically Speaking

How would you describe your voice? Is it mellifluous and pleasant to the ear? Is your delivery clear? Do you enunciate? Is your tone a monotone or do you frequently inflect and vary your pitch? Do you speak enthusiastically? Is your delivery engaging?

Do you say Good Morning, morning, Morning, G'morning, Good MORning, GOOD MORning, Good MorNING, Good MORNING or GOOOOD MORNING?

☼

How *good* does your morning sound?

☼

When asked "How are you?" how enthusiastic are your responses? Let's experiment with these options, which are best said aloud in the company of friends. Feel free to circle the most enchanting options.

☼ *Wonderful, WONderful, WONDERful, WONDERFUL.*

☼ *What a beautiful day. What a BEAUtiful day. WHAT a BEAUtiful DAY. WHAT A BEAUTIFUL DAY.*

☼ *It's so good to see YOU. It's SO good to see you. It's SO GOOD to SEE you. It's so GOOD to see YOU. IT IS SO GOOD TO SEE YOU.*

Enthusiastic delivery improves posture, deepens breathing, opens the heart and brightens the mind. How do *your* body, heart and mind act and feel differently when you pronounce every syllable enthusiastically?

My body…

My heart…

My mind…

Delightful Telephone Greetings

Have you yet tried answering the telephone by saying "Yes! Yes! Yes!"? This glad greeting guarantees a grin, as do oodles of others. For generic joy, I like to answer the phone by saying "Hi Beautiful" to whomever may be calling.

Blissologists avoid answering the phone with a plain "Hello" since the common "Hello" is acoustically comprised of *hell* and *low*, neither of which is highly inspiring. In contrast to "Hello", these *are* inspiring:
Hi how ARE YOU? (asked with caring and without pausing)
Greetings Sunbeam!
Glorious Day, eh?

☼

☼

Bliss Conscious Foods

Challenging it would be to thrive conversationally with someone who is under the influence of heroin. However, the legal poisons that prevail without being queried deeply are possibly as insidious to humanity due to their widespread acceptance.

(Un)natural foods beget (un)natural thoughts, and thoughts are the seedlings of conversations. The more vibrant our foods, the more vibrant are our communication. Offering unwholesome foods to family and friends, including one's self, can derail conversations. Rather than feeding loved ones acceptable toxins such as sugary sweets and caffeinated drinks, what could you serve to inspire the highest quality conversations?

☼

Food is intelligent and inspires intelligence
when consumed in its natural state.

Creating Blissbience: Perfect Places For BCC

Have you ever moved your sofa beside a well-traveled highway so as to better enjoy the splendid, thundering and aromatic conversational ambience? Absurd, isn't it?

The environment is stronger than we are. I find it delightfully humbling that the way we live is greatly influenced by the environment we live in. For example, if we dwell on a tepid island in the tropics, our entire outlook and lifestyle will differ remarkably from when we abide amidst high Himalayan snows.

Myriad non-human factors impact upon our conversational ambience, such as seasons, sunshine, rain, trees, cars, buildings, cultures, languages, laws, media, resources, pollution, peace, proximity to nature and... ☼

Understanding that our environment is stronger than we are, Blissologists, it is essential to create and seek out sanctuaries in our immediate vicinity that exude blissbience, that is, blissful ambience.

Where is the pleasantest place to communicate inside your home, and what makes it particularly so? (Is it deliciously cozy? Is the lighting soft and playful? Does it feature a fabulous painting, an intriguing photograph, an uplifting view or a friendly plant or two? Do family and friends naturally gravitate there and casually sink into the furniture?)

☼

Until relatively recently, nature was the only view available. Today, living near nature is a privilege. In the past, paddling, sailing and walking used to create the moving pictures, as the landscape slowly shifted while the conversationalists starred in every homemade movie.

Even today, walking while talking inspires conversations, especially amidst the company of trees. For countless ages strolling has provided blissbience for rovers, saints and sages. I call this the Jesus technique. To which special places do *you* wander outside your home for fabulous conversations? (When living in cities, cemeteries can be charming.)

☼

How Bliss Conscious Are We?

This list is an easy way to determine our conversational states of being.

The Blissless	The Bliss Conscious
Complain	**Celebrate**
Compete	**Cooperate**
Condemn	**Compliment**
Moan and Whine	**Hum and Sing**
Interrupt	**Breathe and Listen**
Elicit Tears and Frowns	**Elicit Grins**
Bicker	**Create Peace**
Protect themselves	**Protect All**
Dwell in the past and future	**Consciously Live Presently**
Are scattered	**Are Attentive**
Take credit	**Give Credit**
Negatively react	**Positively Respond**
Gossip and slander	**Speak Little and Generously**
Emphasize I, me and mine	**Emphasize We, Us and Ours**
Boast	**Praise**
Rush	**Slow**
Know	**Wonder**
Limit	**Liberate**
Sadden	**Gladden**
Emphasize differences	**Emphasize Commonalities**
Divide	**Unite**
Hear without empathy	**Listen Deeply to Understand**
Like to be right	**Love To Learn**
Fear and shun	**Embrace and Encourage**
Imprison	**Set Free**

Consecrating Conversations

Those who focus on material things grow material minds.
Those who speak about divinity, become divine.

According to your speech, what are you becoming?

☼

If you enjoy discussing inspiring concepts, and you move to a new location, it may feel challenging to initially find people with whom to share. However, such people surround us if only we can discover them. The quality of the questions we ask determines the course of our conversations as well as the degrees of conversational intimacy.

Which intriguing questions would you ask to induce conversations that are deeply meaningful to you?

☼

☼

☼

What is one of your highest spiritual truths?

☼

How do you broaden your spectrum of reality?

☼

Which inspiring insights are you entertaining these days?

☼

Intriguing Questions For Intimates

Be ye joyous unto your beloved.

Is it possible to conversationally approach one's nearest and dearest with perpetual gratitude, awe and wonder? How do *you* inspire playful yet reverent conversational intimacy in *your* closest relationships?

☼

☼

Conversations are either materially or spiritually oriented. How much of your conversations are spiritually focused? During the day do you think of uplifting, thought-provoking, open-ended questions to ask your beloved? If this is not already your habit, create, then ask, one such brilliant question each day, gradually increasing the number of these questions until they comprise the bulk. Which brilliant, uplifting, thought-provoking, open-ended questions would you create as gifts for asking your most intimate associate?

☼

☼

☼

> *How can we deepen sacredness in our communion?*
> *What fosters splendid spontaneity?*
> *What enhances our conversational intimacy?*
> *What are the ways of joyous, peaceful living?*
> *Which ambiences and attitudes encourage creativity?*
> *How can we cultivate ever more bliss in our relationship?*

Unconditionally Wonderful People

At a health retreat recently, a visitor grabbed the hostess's arm then whispered, "I'm a miserable person and you should have nothing to do with me."

"You're a wonderful person," the hostess retorted, fully meaning it.

"Aren't you quick to make a judgment!" snapped the visitor. "You don't even know me. Don't give me that crap."

The hostess responded, *"What you think and say about me and what you think and say about you will not change my opinion. I've made up my mind. You are a wonderful person! I like you. It's that simple, and there's nothing you can do about it."*

A few days later the visitor said "You're my only friend here, and I'd like to give something to you."

"You have," said the hostess.

The Funny Factor for Being Happy In Miserable Moments

Funny isn't it? Here we are in the rain without umbrellas! Without raincoats! Yet endowed with singing voices that could make the thunder listen.

Funny isn't it? Of all the places in the galaxy to rendezvous, *here we are* standing in the same long line at a bank. What a privilege!

In which situations could a splash of gladness brighten the moment?

Funny isn't it?…

Funny isn't it?…

Your Advisory Committee

Character is formed by the company one keeps.

Who are your deepest influences and guides? Who do you emulate and turn to for advice? What specially qualifies them to be deeply respected for their wisdom?

My most important spiritual influences and advisors are:

☼

☼

My career mentors and inspirations are:

☼

☼

My most significant financial guides include:

☼

☼

My most influential relationship role models are:

☼

☼

Do conversations with the special people named above expand your consciousness and catalyse your contentment? Moreover, who comprise your wises associational choices?

☼

☼

Fabulous Farewells

Which phrases do you impart to announce that the moment has now arrived to depart?

☼

The most common good bye is "I have to go now. I need to _____. See you later, bye." Sadly, the "good" part of "good bye" is often omitted. Good-bye originally meant "Go with God", then later "God abide".

How can we generate joy at every parting occasion? Rather than leaving as if each farewell is a small funeral or a petty escape, how can we part affectionately and cheerfully?

ABC's To Cheery Good Byes

Appreciate attentively.
Beam blissings beautifully.
Confirm dreams prophetically.

Appreciate attentively.
What a delightful surprise to share a few moments with you.
It's been a treat to be in your presence.

☼

Beam blissings beautifully.
May indescribable bliss be with you.
May your dream of _____ come true.

☼

Confirm dreams prophetically.
Your future will be fantastic. You will enjoy wonderful times ahead.
Your deep wishes will manifest.

☼

Return Criticisms As Compliments

Do you ever meet people who tend to interpret compliments as criticisms? I decided long ago to interpret all criticisms as compliments, then to return them to their owner. This delightful habit is unbelievably fun.

What could be said if, for instance, someone calls you a rattlesnake? *Thank you! I love rattlesnakes! Rattlesnakes can be gentle, frolicsome and highly telepathic. You are also rattlesnake-esque, so smooth and gorgeous, and that is the highest compliment!"*

Imagine how someone could attempt to criticise you. How could you interpret it as complimentary, then return it to the owner?

☼

☼

Remarkably Good Nights

Wishing someone "Good Night" assists in providing that person with a good night's rest. In this light, which words could convey the most optimum slumber? For example,

Conscious blissful sleep to you.
May you rest amidst angels.
Profound and peaceful sleep be yours.

☼

☼

☼

God night.

The Blisstionary

Dictionaries, like the rest of us, are in perpetual transition. Hence, the advent of The Blisstionary, a dictionary of cheerful, novel concepts for blissological posterity. A wee sampling of blissful conglomerates follows here:

Lortunate - lucky and fortunate. *How lortunate we are to be here.*

Linner - lunch and dinner. *Shall we meet for a linner feast at three?*

Grinoobly - grin and ooh; the feeling of a broad smile coming over ones face for no reasonable reason, and knowing that it is going to grow. *She grew grinoobly while sunbathing amidst wild flowers and butterflies.*

Which of your inventive words would you submit, with definitions and examples, to such a Blisstionary?

☼

☼

☼

Sacred English

Some scholars say Sanskrit is 'the language of holy sounds' and 'the sacred language'. Indeed, all languages are rooted in sounds, hence all languages are rooted in the sacred.

Only recently, since the loss of living near nature, along with the advent of mass secularization and citification, have ancient meanings been twisted, misunderstood and forgotten. Let us savour some of the sacred roots of English.

Samples From the Sacred English Etymology Section Of
The Blisstionary

For Understanding The Original Uplifting Meanings Of Words

Addictions are what we talk to people about. (see page 109)

Attention originated in 'attend' which means to wait and to care for. Attention is the state of caring and waiting upon each passing moment.

Awesome or some awe (-inspiring). Awe means reverence and wonder.

Dife - the totality of death and life, existence and apparent nonexistence

Enthusiastic - those who are enthusiastic are 'in god' because 'en' comes from 'in' and 'thus' is from the Greek god, Theos.

Faith - fate, from the goddess Fates

Forgiving - for giving. Forgiveness is a form of giving and generosity.

Genius - a tutelary deity of ancient times

Good - god

Good-bye – 'god be with you' became 'god abide' became 'good bye'.

Gorgeous - resembling a gorge

Heal - to be whole

Health - wholeness and holiness

Health, Holy and Wholly - share the same root thereby uniting the sacred, holistic and healthful.

Heathen - people who live in the heath

Holy - wholly and healthy

Innocence - inside knowing

Inspire - in spirit

Inspiring - bringing in spirit

Intuition - internal teaching

Invisible - inwardly visible (verses *un*visible as in not at all visible)

Miracle - a visible wonder

Oracle - an audible wonder

Parthenogenesis - biological virgin birth, a common phenomenon among certain insects, lizards, plants and single-celled organisms as well as among some ancient women who practiced it in the Parthenon.

Prosper - 'to make happy' from the Latin verb prosperare. The idea of prospering as material riches was introduced in the English language as slang during the industrial revolution.

Psyche – breath

Queer – mysterious, peculiar, strange

Religion - that to which we give our allegiance again and again

Sacred – holy

Sacrifice - to make sacred

Sacrum - sacred base (of the human body)

Spirit - to breathe from the Latin verb spirare

Surrender - to give up (note: it's not give down)

Tour - turn. The root of *tour* is *turn,* thus a *tour*ist is one who *turns* then re*turns* home. We are all **tourists** on this planet, because the Earth itself is a *tour*ist ceaselessly *tour*ing the solar system, which is *tour*ing the galaxy, which is *tour*ing the universe, which is...

Universe - one word

Weird – wonderful

Wild - willed

☼

☼

We Welcome Your Poetic Licence

You With The Poetic Licence are hereby cordially invited to contribute to The Blisstionary's Creative Phrases Section, which includes, for example:

cloud opera - thunderstorm

Frolicking With Freedom

The very prospect of freedom charms and entices. Most everyone loves feeling free, saying "free" and hearing "free", so feel free to add freely to this free sampling of freedom-enhancing uses of the word free to your freedom-encouraging vocabulary.

carless	☼ **footloose and fancy free**
childless	☼ **childfree and easy on the environment**
deceased	☼ **body free**
divorced	☼ **free**
fruitless	☼ **fruit free**
homeless	☼ **home free, mortgage free, maintenance free**
hopeless	☼ **living in the moment and future free**
hungry	☼ **food free**
irritated	☼ **serenity free**
jobless	☼ **free to be**
penniless	☼ **financially free**
pointless	☼ **point free**
thoughtless	☼ **intellectually unencumbered**
	☼
	☼
	☼

The Importance of Staying Open

A flock of brave souls were having their first lesson in skydiving. One of the students asked, "What if the parachute doesn't open?" "That", explained the instructor, "is what we call jumping to a conclusion."

Epilogue

These amazing times offer abundant opportunities for your special style of Bliss Conscious Communication to continuously evolve. This groundbreaking book is but the beginning of a pristine field of communication with the potential to positively revolutionise the world of inter-relations. The epilogue is yours to discover.

☼

May The Celebration Continue.

Thanks Be To You

Spirit Of The Universe For Ceaseless Surprises, Wondrous Gifts, and Delicious Magic Inherent In Each Moment; For Sacred Silence, Earthlings, Understanding, Moonbeams, Bliss, Energies Within Ethers, Thanks For Writing This. Kudos To You Vortexing Vibrations, Ecstatic Heart Twirls, Children, Chlorophyll Elders, In(wardly)visible Universes, In(wardly)audible Worlds, The Eternally Dancing Light Show of Subatomic Particles, Our Cryptic Beatific Origins, Marvelous Mother, Delightful Dad, Mystic Whispers, Limitless Possibilities, Wizened Trees, Truth, Cotyledons, The Invention Of The Spoon, Fresh Yet Ancient Wind, Dife and Leath, Smiling, Grinning, Nectar Words, Mist, Kindness, Tears, Myriad Tendernesses, Inspiration, Being, Oneness, Whistling Gods, Groovin Goddesses, Mountains, Shiva, Genius, Brooklets, Wildness, Mildness, Meadows, Mosquitoes, Deep Peace, Fauna Families All, Singing Passerines, Siblings Submarine, Rainbows Everywhere, Tingling in Perpetual Awe, Attention Crystalline, The Capacity To Wonder, Inspired Creativity, Devotion, Giggling, Bodhisattvas, Bhajans, Blossoming, Twilight, Transmutation, Satsang, Skipping, Satyavan, Singing, Offering, Compassion, Peace, Internal Paradises, Havens Of Well-Being, Revelations, Illumination, Emerald Seas, Idiosyncrasies, Sacred Forests, Now Sweet Now, Sweet Is The Living Loving Universe, The Humble Miracle Called Soil, and Sangha, Compost For The Soul. Moreover Thanks Be To Sooo Many Homo Sapient Sisters…Generous Judy, Metta Anna, Angelic Debra, Cheery Hannah, Sprouting Molly, Michelle the Prodigy, Kali Agnus, Kirtana, Jenny, Love Is Sara, Unconditional Ola, Starburst Sophie, Effervescent Manawa, Very Viv, YouAreIt Ateeka… And Chinese Hai Ming Which Means "Sunlight Shimmering On The Sea". Thanks Be To You Four Billion Human Brothers Bob, Rob, Mystical Milton, Amazing Mukesh, Shaman Michael, Loving Len, Mohammed Edrees, Happy Jack, Brilliant Tim, Joy Called John, Chortling Jeffry, Sadhu Dave, Roger Rajananda, Ethereal Paul, Swami Phil, And Inspiring Wayne, All Wise and Loving Sadhus, Sages, Aspirants, Mystics, Ascetics, Gurus, and Hermits, Faerie Friends, Elements, Families, Beings And Nonbeings, All Past-Present-Future Time-Spaceless Precious Beings Inclusive You, All Rainbows In A Drop Of Dew And First and Most and Last of All Cosmic Conscious Blissful Love Which Sustains Us.

Thanks Be To You

Index of The Blissiplines

A Special Request

Dear Blissologist,

It's been pure pleasure co-creating this with *you*! I am particularly pleased to be meeting people such as you, who are dedicated to broadcasting joy into the world.

In some situations, happiness has become an endangered species. Together we can bring happiness to the fore by starting a worldwide revolution of smiles, one conversation at a time.

Would you like to share your related inspirations, personal conversational testimonies, comments about this book, and humorous anecdotes with the author? If so, wonderful! Galaxies of gratitude to you. Your ideas will be gratefully acknowledged in the enhanced, greatly expanded, forthcoming edition.

Myriad Blissings,

Happy

Other Books by Happy Oasis

Uncivilized Ecstasies

Choosing To Be Childless

Learning To Live Like A Mammal

Yoga In Bed: *Asanas For Cozy Yogis*

The Vibrant Vegan: *Raw Recipes For Radiant Health*

An Invitation From The Author

Now that we've become friends, it would be wonderful to cultivate your acquaintance. You are welcome to visit the author in paradise. Happy's Haven of Well-Being is a private residential beachfront island retreat for reconnection, relaxation and rejuvenation. For fabulous retreat photographs and depictions, email happyatthehaven@xtra.co.nz
Enquire there as well for books, retreat reservations, health vacations, Bliss Conscious Communication Events, Bliss Facilitators' Training Weekends (Yes, You can become a Certified Blissologist), Solar Yoga, Meniscus Meditations, Sacred Sharing Circles, Vibrant Vegan Feasts, Music Moondays, art exhibitions, special gatherings and ongoing personal retreats at both The Haven of Well-Being and in The Sacred Forest, an alpine conservation of ancient trees.

Happy Oasis
happyatthehaven@xtra.co.nz
The Haven of Well-Being
Tryphena RD 1
Great Barrier Island
New Zealand
(09) 4290 122

Help us broadcast the bliss by giving gifts of Bliss Conscious Communication to families, friends, 'enemies', libraries, companies, colleges, curmudgeons and other precious loved ones. We appreciate you and your spirit of generosity! In an effort to share the bliss, we offer bulk book order discounts. Just ask. Let's legalise happiness. Kindly include $29.95 plus $3 shipping per copy. Thanks be to you.

This is not a silly book.
Happiness is a serious career.

Our happiness must be deep enough
Our lives must be honest enough
Our speech generous enough
To prevent quarrels
Which culminate in violence
And the subsequent suffering
of innocent lives.

Today may we be happy stuff
aware enough to prevent strife.
May we grin today for harmony
And giggle together for world peace.

The Beginning